Mesmerism in Connection with Popular Superstitions

by J.W. Jackson

with an introduction by Dahlia V. Nightly

CREDITS & ACKNOWLEDGEMENTS

Front Cover -
St. Francis Borgia Helping a Dying Impenitent (Circa 1788)
by Francisco Goya (1746-1828)
[Public Domain],
From the *Colección Marquesa de Santa Cruz* (Madrid, España).
via Wikimedia Commons

Back Cover -
Maria von Mörl by Luigi Gonzaga Giuditti / Louis Gaston de Ségur (1820-1881)
Color digitally enhanced by Black Books
[Public Domain],
*via Wikimedia Common*s

Black Books Logo -
Candle Collection by VectorPocket, via FreePik.com *(Cropped)*
Vanitas [Painting] by Bartholomäus Bruyn the Elder, Public Domain *(Cropped)*
Marbled Pedestal with Old Books by Kues1, via FreePik.com (Cropped)

Research / Sources -
Wikimedia Commons
www.Commons.Wikimedia.org

Many thanks to all the incredible photographers, artists,
researchers, and archivists who share their great work.

PLEASE NOTE :
As with all reprinted books of this age that are intended to perfectly reproduce the
original edition, considerable pains and effort had to be undertaken to correct fading and
sometimes outright damage to existing proofs of this title. At times, this task can be quite
monumental, requiring an almost total rebuilding of some pages from digital proofs of
multiple copies. Despite this, imperfections still sometimes exist in the final proof and
may detract slightly from the visual appearance of the text.

DISCLAIMER :
Due to the age of this book, some methods or practices may have been deemed unsafe or
unacceptable in the interim years. In utilizing the information herein, you do so at your
own risk. We republish antiquarian books without judgment or revisionism, solely for
their historical and cultural importance, and for educational purposes.

Black Books
PUBLICATIONS

Introduction

Here at *Black Books* we are so happy to bring you this special edition of an incredible old find on Mesmerism and its related themes.

This special edition of **Mesmerism in Connection With Popular Superstitions** was written by J.W. Jackson, and first published in 1858, making it over 160 years old.

This antiquarian text features sections on *Charms – Amulets, Chrystallic Divination, and Magic Mirrors, Witchcraft, Exorcism, Magic, and Enchantment, Village Ghosts and Fairies, Stigmata and Crown of Glory, Death Omens,* and more.

The book features several religion-related sections with subjects like Stigmatics, Visions, Miracles and Papal Ritual.

This fantastic old find is an absolute must-have for all those interested in the history of Superstition and its related subjects including Divination, the Dark Arts, Religious Experiences, and the Supernatural.

Strangely yours...

~ Dahlia V. Nightly

State of Jefferson, July 2018

CONTENTS.

INTRODUCTION,

THIS is an age of resurrection. We are exhuming the past,
and evoking its long-buried records, and darkly concealed
knowledges from the tomb. Egypt at our mighty invocation
has yielded up the secret of her hieroglyphics, while at the
same potent spell, Nineveh and Babylon have surrendered
the chronicles engraved on the arrow headed tablets of their
ruined palaces. The higher creed of Brahma and the deeper
faith of Budha, with all the mystic grandeur and profound
significance of Oriental theosophy, are opening to us, like some
long-locked treasury, of which the subtle magician intellect has
found the key; and we stand trembling and aghast, at the
splendour of our discovery, and the greatness of our possessions.
From the grass-grown sepulchres of Europe's Allophyllian abo-
rigines to the collossal piles of the Thebaid, and from the
ruined cities of central America to the rock-hewn temples of
Hindostan, the gone is again becoming vocal, and like a
royal spirit at the behest of some mighty enchanter, reveals
to us at once, the legend of its glory and the record of its
crimes. We are thus brought face to face with the sublimest
ages of antiquity. We are privileged in these latter days to
behold unveiled the moral physiognomy of those heroic
generations, to whose labours and aspirations, humanity is
indebted for the commencement of civilization and the dawn
of knowledge. We are ascending to the well-springs of intelligence, and drawing inspiration from those divine fountains, whence the men of primitive times derived their

wondrous grandeur of thought, and their as yet, unequalled sublimity of conception.

We are becoming wiser and therefore humbler. The ignorant and unthinking may still prattle like nursery babes about the signs of progress, and fancy that there never was a century of light, till that of the nineteenth happily dawned on a benighted world. But better informed and more reflective minds are beginning to confess, that, while we have undoubtedly discovered much and achieved more, while we have accumulated facts, and applied them with unparalleled energy and assiduity to the practical requirements of life, in these modern experimental ages, we have also in our all-absorbing devotion to the inductive philosophy, overlooked and forgotten much that was of priceless value in the systems and tuitions of our predecessors, and that our disintegrative criticism and destructive analysis, constitute, after all, an inferior phase of developement, to the creative power and reconstructive synthesis of a preceding and mightier era. We have no doubt wisely descended from principle to fact, from law to phenomena, from heaven to earth. We have left " the old high, *à priori* road," of theory, for the lower and safer, *a posteriori*, path of careful investigation, but let us never forget that this was a *descent*. We have broken the rock into fragments, and ground the latter into sand, and rejoice in the multiplicity and diversity of our acquisitions; forgetting that one Titanic sum total, may outweigh an indefinite accumulation of little items.

The majesty of the past is being recognized. It is well, for out of this filial reverence, will in due time arise a corresponding royalty in the future. The age of scepticism is on the wane. The waters of unbelief are on the ebb. The epoch of doubt is drawing to a close, and that of true poetic recreation and belief is already mantling like a moral daydawn in the rosy east. Foremost among these more cheering characteristics of our age, is the re-appearance of mesmerism, denuded of its needless accessories as a superstition, and becoming gradually clothed in the sober vestments of truth, as

a science.   A sacred lore derived from the primeval ages,—a
mystic knowledge, cradled in India, nursed in Egypt, and
templed in Greece, yet long despised in modern Europe, its
gradual recognition as a department of the experimental
philosophy, is an important fact, whose significance cannot
well be over-estimated.   As a tidal mark, it shows that the
returning flood of faith, is again covering the shallows of
infidelity with its deep and holy waters.   As the restoration
of a long-lost and neglected branch of knowledge, it indicates
the approach of that grander age of universality, when the old
and the new, the wisdom of the past and the knowledge of the
present, shall combine to produce a future grander than either.

Of its medical utilities, and consequent demand on the
kindly consideration of the philanthropist, I have elsewhere
spoken.   Of its relationship to metaphysical investigation, I
intend hereafter to speak.   My more especial purpose now,
is to demonstrate its presence as a fact in nature, existing
beneath the figments of popular belief in the preternatural, to
show that it was the enduring substance, of which superstition
is but the passing shadow.   Operating by an imponderable
force invisible to all but lucid extatics, yet productive of
effects perceptible to the rudest, it is no wonder that its processes were regarded as necromantic, and its results supposed
to be the effects of sorcery.   Known in its higher departments
only to a sacredly initiated few, by whom this mystic lore
was religiously preserved from the profane vulgar, it was almost unavoidable that the latter should be impressed with
the idea of supernatural agency, and so conceive of rare
phenomena as special miracles.   As effects to whose
spontaneous production, unassisted nature is everywhere competent, many of its most striking wonders have been moreover
frequently manifested through the instrumentality of agents,
themselves ignorant of the power with which they were endued, and so misapprehending the force which they exerted.
Such were oftentimes the seers and thaumaturgists of antiquity; not conscious impostors, but high-wrought enthusiasts: not deceivers, but, if you will, fanatics.

It must not be supposed that these few letters exhaust the subject; on the contrary, they barely indicate it. Tradition is a rich mine, a very gold-field of buried knowledge, in whose auriferous sands the slowly accumulated wealth of ages lies hidden. The past generations were not wholly foolish, although modern superficiality may refuse to recognise a wisdom too profound for its shallow appreciation. Our forefathers saw nature face to face quite as nearly, and perhaps quite as clearly as ourselves. If their eyes were shut to some things, on whose perception we so especially value ourselves, they were open to others in reference to which we are proportionately blind. If they were be-clouded, and so misled by superstition, we are equally darkened and misdirected by prejudice. And of the two evils, it is perhaps the lesser, to see a phenomenon with open eyes, although we afterwards misapprehend its character, then to be so hood-winked by preconceptions, as to refuse the evidence of nature, although she come into court with what should be the irresistible demonstration of fact. It is not my purpose, however, to tire the reader's patience and weary his attention by the vague platitudes of an introduction. The letters will speak for themselves. They were written for the purpose of elucidating a profoundly interesting province of human experience, and are now published in the hope of directing the attention of thinking minds, to a comparatively new and instructive subject of contemplation, in whose investigation they cannot fail to discover many things little dreamed of, in the very practical philosophy of matter and motion.

I have not in these pages treated of mesmerism in its elementary principles. The reader will find here, neither a connected description of its scientific phenomena, nor an attempted exposition of their causes. For this I must refer him to my "Lectures on Mesmerism," of which this work may be considered as a continuation. Here much is taken for granted, or is supposed to be understood, of which the demonstration and explanation are to be found elsewhere. These letters, in short, pre-suppose a certain acquaintance with mesmerism on the part of those who peruse them. This was unavoidable in a production constituting one of a series, in which my object is to develope sequentially the principles of a profound and arcane lore, and lead the reader step by step to their grander application. Hence I have purposely avoided even a condensed recapitulation of facts and laws, respecting which, a sufficiency of information, for an instructive perusal of the present, may be found in a preceding treatise. Finally, let not the spirit in which I have penned these pages be misapprehended. There is in them a loyalty to the truth, an allegiance which should be paramount; but there is no intentional hostility to any sect or party. I have written from my convictions, and if these be based on misconception and error, though others may perceive their inaccuracy, I at least can vouch for their honesty.

LETTER FIRST.

CHARMS, AMULETS, CHRYSTALLIC DIVINATION, AND MAGIC MIRRORS.

AT all periods of time, in addition to the established or orthodox system of belief, men have shown a tendency to put faith in something extraneous and additional, generally embodied in tales of the supernatural, which the less credulous of their contemporaries or the more wise of their posterity have termed superstition. This, when historically investigated, is often found to be but the faded relic of some antecedent but supplanted religion, not the less potent however, on this account with the masses, nor, we may add, the less terrible to the susceptible. Such were the magic, sorcery and witchcraft of bygone ages, with their divinations, enchantments, and invocations. Such are the ghost stories, rappings, presentiments, prophetic dreams, and other forms of heterodox belief, which in the faintest attenuation still survive to our own time. Anathematised as diabolical at one period and ridiculed as non-existent at another, now employed as motive forces in the management of mighty empires, and then treated as a stock subject for the banter of the polite, the wondrous phenomena evolved through the occult sciences, and developed under interior illumination, have been subjected to a contrasted but generally unfavourable fate. Regarded as too sacred for philosophic investigation in the earlier ages, and too contemptible for serious notice in later times, these strange revelations of usually latent force have been hitherto, as by universal consent, abandoned to the practice of the mystical and the belief of the ignorant. Rejected as apocryphal because too marvellous for reception by modern historians, the narratives of ancient thaumaturgy have slumbered unnoticed amidst the record of antecedent eras.

whose oracles and prodigies have excited not an enlightened spirit of investigation but a supercilious and ignorant contempt, that discrediting such effects, also disdained to inquire into their causes. We have now, however, thanks to a more ex pansive philosophy and a more enlightened antiquarianism, passed this period of unreflecting indiffereuce, and the super- stitions of the past are beginning to be contemplated as an invaluable storehouse of physiological and psychological facts, waiting only the discriminating investigation of properly qualified minds to yield a rich supply of invaluable results. And it is admitted by all who have paid any serious attention to this most interesting department of inquiry, that mesmerism affords the most satisfactory, and we might say, indeed, the only efficient key to these long transmitted and venerable mysteries. Its experiments alone enable us to illustrate the recorded facts which, without the light cast on them by its now well ascertained phenomena, would apparently remain for ever an utterly insoluble problem. Nor is this to be wondered at. Ages of tradition necessarily find those of creation inexplicable. We have on all moral subjects lived so long and so luxuriously in those sublime structures of thought which our more energetic predecessors built up, that looking upon their vast and awe-inspiring proportions, we are ever ready to exclaim, in conscious impotency, like Turks amidst the glorious ruins of Hellas, " they are the work not of mortals but Titans, they are founded not on fact but miracle, and were created, not by perishing men but deathless spirits."

But to descend from these rather towering flights to the details of our interesting theme. No humanitarian tradition, no universal belief ever yet rested on a nonentity. The long enduring must have a truth in it, for lies ever tend to that whence they came—nothing. Now, taking them as a whole, mankind have always believed in the preter, and we might say, indeed, the supernatural; and this, too, not only as a past and defunct, but also as a present and existing manifestation. Only in ages of lamentable dilapidation and spiritual death unutterable, when faith has receded into the innermost chambers of the soul, have men ever come definitively to the conclusion that marvels had ceased, and were no longer among the things extant in God's creation. And truly a most sorrowful time it is, when such infidelity supervenes, and brings with it a night-time, in which all the nearer glories of the universe are obscured, and the wayfarer groping in darkness, directs his course as best he may by lights removed to a well-nigh incalculable distance. Fortunately such periods have ever been but the precursors of a still brighter illumination—that gloomiest of hours which precedes the radiance of impending morn. Now, out of such a time are we just emerging; those mountain tops, our loftiest intellects, being as yet alone bathed in the ruddy glory of the coming day. And to what, humanly speaking, do we owe this deliverance from a worse than Egyptian bondage? In part, undoubtedly, to the advances of that very philosophy which till of late so comfortably reposed on its matter and its machinery. We have passed from the ponderable to the imponderable sphere of investigation, and ascended from corporeal to mental phenomena, as subject-matter for experiment; and instead of foolishly denying well-authenticated results, because unaccountable on received hypotheses, have at last condescended to test the evidence of their existence, and admit them within the category of established facts, not for their probability but their reality.

Shall we then endeavour, as far as may be, to account for the existence of processes once generally adopted, and of credences once widely received, by showing that the appearances on which they challenged the respect and belief of mankind were not fallacious but genuine; not the products of imposture, but the necessary effects of natural though misapprehended forces. As we proceed, it will become obvious that not only were mankind at one period extensively devoted to the practice of mesmerism as an occult art, but that they still are so, the traditional form having survived till the scientific phase supervened, so that the silvery thread of this bright and beautiful knowledge has passed on unbroken from the primeval to the present generation, and will now in all probability, so descend increasingly to the final, the noblest heritage of lore which any age has ever bequeathed to its successor. We will then commence with the simpler, and so gradually ascend to the more recondite and profound of those processes, which were once deemed appropriate instrumentalities for evoking spiritual forces into operative manifestation. And first as to charming for curative purposes. What can be less imposing, we might almost say more contemptible in appearance, than the mumbled chant and superstitiously limited strokings of the village crone? And yet, even in this faint record of ancient hygeian practice, we may distinctly trace the existence of mesmerism under its antique form. Those strokings are passes, that mumbling is for the purpose of sustaining and concentrating the attention of an otherwise undisciplined mind on the matter in hand, and that old man or woman is a far-off disciple of the once powerful priesthood of Æsculapius and Isis, of Vishnu and Mithras. The thing is now in its sear and yellow leaf, more especially in the West, but follow it up to its primitive home in the East, trace it back to its ages of greatness even here, and behold that power which, however ridiculous now, was once the richly-prized heritage of Celtic Druids, and Teutonic priests of Odin. Read the lines of Solon and Martial in reference to these very passes; investigate the frictional processes employed by the classic Æsclepiadæ; behold the favourite positions of Egyptian, Assyrian, and Hindoo divinities; and you will at once perceive that this simple peasant has inherited the weak and faded remnant of a lore once cultured amidst all the grandeur of antiquity's Hygeian temples, and supported by all the pomp and circumstance of their attendant priesthood.

In addition to this direct application of the power, which would imply the personal attendance of the medical, who was generally also the sacerdotal operator, the ancients were and the orientals still are accustomed to transmit mesmeric influence through the medium of a great variety of substances, to be subsequently taken as medicines or worn as amulets. The operator who has observed the effect of mesmerised water on his patient, will be at no loss to understand the general belief once prevalent in the efficacy of charmed or blessed medicaments, nor will any one who has seen a handkerchief made the vehicle of mesmeric influence be altogether incapable of comprehending the widespread faith, which once existed, in the potency of certain articles supposed also to be sanctified. Neither will any one, acquainted with what a good clairvoyante can accomplish by a lock of hair, be at a loss to understand how the veriest shreds and patches of a saint should be religiously preserved after his death as priceless treasures. A reverence for relics, although no doubt turned to an especially good account by the Budhistic lamas of the East and the Romish priests of the West, is nevertheless based on something more venerable than the system of either, namely, on the laws of nature. The reliance once placed on the virtues of precious stones no doubt rested in part on the *od* force, which the Baron Von Reichenbach has discovered to be especially resident in crystals, and which is perhaps the origin of their being worn at present as mere ornaments. Of old, however, they were regarded as talismans, and as such were generally covered with mystic signs or inscriptions, supposed to be indicative of, if not contributive to, their especial virtues. To understand, perhaps, is better than to abuse these things, and the enlightened philosophy which can explain may do as much to banish such superstitions as the ignorant zeal which can only condemn, for an age like our own demands not only eloquent declamation but also philosophic investigation.

This, then, brings us to divination by the crystal, the instruments for which are occasionally exhumed from the catacombs of Egypt, and which is still practised in the secret chambers of Grand Cairo, while the evidences of its existence are not wanting in the remains of Nineveh and Babylon, nor have its processes yet become obsolete on the banks of the Euphrates or the Tigris. It still lingers, indeed, as an interesting relic of former times from Pekin to London, and its devotees are perhaps scarcely less numerous in modern

Lancashire than in ancient Assyria. On what fact in nature, then, is this hallucination based, on what small basis of reality has this mighty superstructure of fantasy been erected? On the fact that by gazing steadily at and into a sphere of glass or a drop of inky fluid, certain naturally susceptible persons become so far mesmerised as to be partially lucid, in which state they see visions akin to those of a mesmeric clairvoyante. A crystal seer is indeed simply an ecstatic, whose nervous system has become preternaturally exalted in its functions, and who consequently is capable of achieving all those feats which have been attributed to either spontaneously developed or mesmeric lucides. The tales of jewelled rings worn by royal and other personages of distinction, and which were said to have the property of turning colour at, or in some other way indicating the approach of poison, seem to be based on a vague misconception of the powers supposed to be resident in the magic crystal, among which prevision and thought-reading were usually numbered, the preventative character of which, in relation to intended or impending evil, would naturally cause the instrumentalities through which such gifts could be more especially exercised to be highly valued.

We have said that this ancient form of divination is not yet extinct even in Britain. It seems, indeed, to have recently undergone a revival, and while sedulously cultivated among the operatives of our manufacturing districts, is not altogether unknown among the more refined but not less wonder-loving dwellers in Belgravia. Now, as a department of the experimental philosophy, as an additional means for investigating the nature and extent of mesmeric susceptibility or the power and quality of the *od* force, these gazings and the visions to which they give birth are profoundly interesting to the most enlightened mind, and ought to appear quite unexceptionable even to the most scrupulous. But when the process itself is seriously introduced as a forbidden art, and the objects seemingly beheld in the crystal are vaunted as actual revelations from the spirit sphere, the subject assumes a graver aspect, for so exercised it may conduce to the formation of very erroneous ideas in reference either to faith or practice. How, then, is the good to be secured and the evil to be avoided? By absurdly ignoring the facts, and declaring that they really do not exist, or by still more foolishly attributing them to the devil, or at all events to some spiritual influence good or bad? Most assuredly not. To deny the existence of the visions would be simply to expose our ignorance of the subjective experience of all susceptible persons who have made the experiment, while to attribute them to preternatural agency is to commit the error of antecedent ages, when all the rarer and more striking phenomena of nature were supposed to result from direct spiritual intervention. It only remains, then, for men of science to courageously investigate the essential character of the phenomena, and while thus asserting their just claims to be esteemed the interpreters of nature, they will at the same time provide a safeguard against those outbursts of fanaticism among the ignorant, which are ever to be feared when seemingly inexplicable facts are presented to their notice as the undoubted results of supernatural forces. I am most happy to find that a commencement has been already made in the right direction, and I have no doubt that by due perseverance in the institution of such experiments on the power of crystals to evoke lucid vision, as some of those narrated by Dr Gregory in his profoundly interesting letters, we shall eventually attain not only to a more accurate knowledge respecting the *odic* property of various substances in nature, and their relationship to the nervous system of man, but also to what is perhaps far more valuable, a clearer insight into the latent capabilities of the human mind, and the laws which regulate the seeming transference of phenomena from the subjective to the objective sphere.

Of all the pleasing traditions which have descended to us in connection with the superstitious practices of other ages, few are so rich in artistic association, or so redolent of the romance of youthful and ardent affection, as the magic mirrors of mediaeval necromancers.   These strange old sorcerers were not always vulgar quacks and ignorant impostors ; on the contrary, they were often men deeply versed in the occult lore of their times, and with a sufficiency of scholastic culture, to redeem them from the contempt even of professed students. Devoted more especially to scientific investigation, they were generally far gone in the pursuit of an *elixir vitae* that promised their gray hairs a prospective immortality of renovated youth and beauty, or were hopelessly involved in a search for the philosopher's stone, which should redeem their poverty, by the mutation of copper into gold at some happily chosen moment of successful projection.   They were enthusiasts, mistaken perhaps as to their means, and in error as to the results which they anticipated, but they were neither so contemptible intellectually or so detestible morally, as might be supposed from the degraded condition of the few miserable creatures who still attempt the prosecution of pursuits, which society has long since outgrown and ignored.   Let us for a short time withdraw the veil of intervening centuries, and behold one of these mysterious beings with his processes and accessories, and after having contemplated the picture, we will attempt its explanation.

A gallant and chivalrous youth long absent in war or on travel, hears during his sojourning in foreign lands, of some potent enchanter, who by the mysterious might of his terrible spells, can evoke a spiritual presentment of any loved and worshipped object, though dwelling afar off in the distant fatherland of the anxious inquirer.   With firm and unhesitating step, yet with bounding pulse, the ardent and excited lover, wrapped in his military cloak, and relying on the shadows of advancing night to screen him yet more effectually from impertinent observation, seeks that sombre house in a retired street of the fortified cathedral city, with its narrow lanes, lofty gables and projecting eaves. He knocks, again and again, at the low but strongly framed oaken door, which is at length slowly unbarred and opened by an old fashioned and trusty domestic, after befitting colloquy with whom, he is at length ushered into the very presence-chamber of the master. To the due adornment of this sanctum of the occult, astrology and alchymy have lent the combined aid of all their mystic signs and manifold appliances. Alembics, astrolabes, vellum-covered volumes, suspicious looking vials, and half-completed horoscopes, are mingled in most admired confusion with stuffed alligators and defunct tortoises. These however are the mere framework of the picture, or, shall we say, its deeply-shaded background, intended to bring out in full relief, by the well-arranged light of that aromatic lamp, the strangely impressive and almost commanding figure of the venerable magician, constituting in himself a more nearly insoluble problem and inscrutible mystery, than any or all the remaining objects in his curiously furnished apartment. His flowing robes of oriental fashion are confined by a girdle of " virgin parchment," on which the signs of the Zodiac are beautifully traced in red and gold. His silvery locks fall from beneath a richly jewelled cap of purple velvet, and his snowy beard sweeps the Zodiacal insignia at his waist. There is power in that lofty brow, penetration in that searching eye, delicacy in that finely chisselled nose, and decision in those firmly closed lips. Intellect has lit up these magnificently moulded features as with the well-ripened glory of a setting sun, and over the strongly marked lineaments of this majestic countenance, age has diffused the calm serenity as of an autumnal eve. It is a face that once seen can never be forgotten, with its expression of sublime repose and exalted meditation, dwelling at an immeasurable altitude above the common-place topics and trifling occasions of ordinary life. Such, alas, was but too often the fantastic vesture of mediaeval genius, stooping through an untoward destiny in its declining years, to the practice of popular magic for a subsistence.

But to proceed with our narrative. The request of the stranger is soon preferred, and the consent of the necromancer, after a little politic hesitation on his part, ultimately obtained. Fasts and vigils are imposed on the consulting neophyte, whose nervous system is thus prepared for a lucid crisis, to which overstrained expectancy and ardent affection, also contribute their by no means insignificant aid. These preliminaries being settled, another meeting is appointed on a day astrologically suitable, when the anticipated spiritual interview is promised, provided the supernal powers prove propitious. For this all the manifold resources of occult art are put into requisition. The magician is endued in his most imposing robe, and has on his breast a talisman of wondrous and unsearchable power. While on every finger of the hand wherewith he waves his mystic rod of invocation, is a jewelled amulet of such protective efficacy, as to defy the combined assaults of all the legions of pandemonium. A ponderous volume, consisting of choice spells and invocations, lies open on an elevated reading desk, near which a chafing dish, resting on a classical tripod, emits ever and anon the fumes of an agreeable yet subtle incense. In case of need, a silver beaker of aromatic wine, to whose preparation alchymy has lent its most potent aid, is placed ready for the support of the agitated and almost fainting disciple. All is now ready. The sorcerer, in a solemn monotone, reads spell after spell from his magical breviary. The gracefully arranged drapery, which had previously covered one side of the room, is slowly withdrawn, and reveals a clear and highly polished mirror, which it had previously veiled. In a short time, a mist from the incense in the chafing dish gradually collects, the odorous volumes thickening and settling into ever increasing density. The reading ceases, and notes of low and distant music falls sweetly on the ear, wearied by previous monotony. The necromancer signs to the startled inquirer, that he may now advance to within a stated distance of the mirror, from which with every wave of his magic wand, the mist gradually disappears, revealing like the moon from behind a retreating cloud, the lovely form of a young and beautiful girl, calmly slumbering in maiden innocence on a graceful couch. There can be no deception .It is herself. The more than eagle-glance of love can detect no difference between this wierd semblance and the well-remembered reality. She lives. The snowy bosom rising and falling with every respiration, now heaves as with some agitating dream. The ruby lips part as in attempted utterance. Her eyelids, with their long and silken auburn lashes quiver in approaching vigilance. She wakes. Their glances meet. Her arms are extended. It is too much for mortality to endure any longer, and the thoughtless youth, breaking through every prescribed rule, rushes to the mirror with a torrent of endearing and tender epithets. Alas for the ardour of passion when opposed to the coolness of science. The seeming reality fades at once into nonentity, every vestige of the delightful vision, dissolving and vanishing like the phantoms of a dream before the light of returning con- sciousness. What a contrast between the benevolent smile of the calm and self-possessed enchanter, and the agonized look of the bereaved and disconsolate lover. Gentle re- proofs from the one, and wild reproaches from the other, ending in friendly explanation, conclude the strange and unearthly scene, from whence the young traveller departs, amazed, confounded, and awe-stricken, a believer in magic for the remainder of his life. Such, with some slight modi- fications, was the psychic interview of our own gallant and accomplished Surrey with the spirit of his fair Geraldine, he being then on a tour in Italy, and she re- siding at home in her own "merry England." And such, we may add, were also the experiences of tens of thousands of other gallant and accomplished gentlemen, both of his own and of many preceding ages.

Now what were the facts in nature underlying this wierd presentment of the seemingly preternatural ? What were the substantive realities on which, as a foundation, this idealized superstructure of pleasing phantasmata was so successfully reared ? Had the alchymical old sage any real power over the spirit of the lady, or was the whole affair but a common- place trick of " natural magic," that is, a mere optical delu- sion ? Neither the one nor the other, we reply. It was simply a biological experiment, effected with many cumbrous if not needless accessories, yet nevertheless eventuating successfully. The image of the lady dwelt in the "mind's eye" of her devoted lover, and the real art of the enchanter, consisted in his power of projecting this subjective conception into apparently objective visibility on the mirror. His fame, his costume, and his apartment, were appliances with which to produce the requisite force of impression. The fasts, the vigils, and the medicated incense, were means for inducing a requisite amount of susceptibility in his subject. Such a potent combination of exciting and évocative influences could scarcely fail to result in vision. The proportion of failures must have been small, and when they occurred could be easily accounted for on astrological, magical, and other sources of defect, including some personal and especial disqualification on the part of the enquirer, for sharing in such exalted and supersensuous investigations. That occasionally cases of true lucidity would be developed under such circumstances is not only probable, but certain. These, however, would constitute the exceptions, and would bear but a small proportion to those of a biological order. That in a few still rarer class of instances, where antecedent interspheration had prepared the way for such a result, the lady herself might be thrown into the transe-sleep by such intensity of feeling and fixity of attention on the part of her lover is also possible, in which case on a subsequent comparison of notes, it would be found they were both simultaneously affected with visional extacis, in virtue of which, each might obtain cognition of the other's actual occupation at the moment. Of this psychic interaction between two profoundly intersphered beings, the drama has skilfully availed itself in the Corsican brothers, whose mutual apparition, when produced with proper stage-effect, is always a source of such thrilling interest to the spectator. Such then were the magic mirrors of mediæval and more remote antiquity. They were biological instrumentalities of a powerful order, but the results which they produced never transcended any natural laws, and were such as are still easily reproducible under the necessary conditions.

LETTER SECOND.

SEERDOM AND ORACLES.

HAVING now entered on the subject of ancient supernaturalism as a belief founded to a considerable extent on mesmeric facts, misapprehended as to their essential character, and consequently misinterpreted in their relationship to man and his destiny, I now purpose going more at length into the detail of this profoundly interesting department of inquiry. We have already seen in charming and divination by the crystal, some of the lower stages of that mystic art, by which it was once supposed that men could place themselves in direct communication with a supersensuous sphere of being, and when necessary, employ its tremendous potencies for their own convenience. It has been already remarked that the wonderful has ever more charms than the useful, and we must not be astonished, therefore, that the exaltation of clairvoyance should have been generally employed for vaticination ; nor ought it to excite much surprise that even the therapeutic practice of mesmerism should have assumed the form of exorcism for the expulsion of devils. Once grant, indeed, that the power used is preternatural, and men, as by a logical sequence, arrive at the conclusion that its effects cannot be properly placed within the category of ordinary phenomena. Once fully persuaded that they are on " the night side of nature," and everything, being viewed through the medium of this impression, assumes a weird and spectral aspect, till at length the most common-place facts are taken for portentous prodigies, and anything at all uncommon is at once considered to be especially miraculous. And when we consider that even in our own days there are not wanting a considerable number of even well-informed individuals who attribute mesmeric results to diabolic agency, we must not be too hasty in condemning earlier generations for arriving at a similar conclusion. However absurd now, it was comparatively rational then, although amidst the light of modern science such opinions are indicative of little else than the imbecility or bigotry of those who are so foolish as to entertain them.

Of all the proclivities of the human mind, none perhaps is stronger than that which prompts it to penetrate into the unknown, and of this undiscovered realm the future seems to be the most attractive province. Hence, in all ages men have attempted to lift the veil which, under ordinary circumstances, separates them with its impenetrable foldings from to-morrow. In modern times this is accomplished to some extent by science, and the astronomer foretells, with mathematical precision, the occurrence of an eclipse, and the pathless ocean can be traversed like a village green, in full reliance on the regular advent of those precalculated occultations, whose time informs the adventurous mariner of his place upon the trackless wilderness of waters. This is our astrology stripped of its adventitious accessories, and reduced to the simple yet awe-inspiring grandeur of inductive knowledge. But who shall say that the unvarying order of astral phenomena, with their majestic cycles, so superior to all the disturbing influences of mundane affairs, so accurately recurrent at mighty intervals, did not afford some excuse for that most sublime of all the aberrations of devotion, the sabeism of the eastern magi, and that grandest of all the processes of vaticination—the attempt to deduce the forthcoming events of human destiny from movements known to be precalculable, and of whose methodic arrival the experience of ages showed no doubt could be entertained. We have now separated fact from fiction—thanks to the labour of forty centuries; but the error preceded the truth and led the way to it:

> " The darkness first and then the light
>   Is God's unerring plan ;
>   His actions have proclaimed it right,
>   Submit, then, mortal man."—*M.S.*

But while our remote predecessors were thus engaged in looking abroad upon the universe without for aids to anticipation, and groping darkly therein, as creatures fitted for the radiance of spirit always will do, amidst the adumbrations of matter, they discovered a fountain within, whose light, especially for the distant and the future, promised to far transcend anything obtainable from extraneous sources. They found that man, amidst the ruins of a mighty nature, still preserved deeply buried under the coarseness of his material envelopment, and fearfully beclouded amidst the darkness of his merely sensuous life, that remnant of his celestial origin, that faint tracery of a long past impress once divine—the gift of seer power, the fragment of that mastery of time, which constituted perhaps a portion of his primal but forfeited inheritance. Finding that this interior illumination occasionally manifested itself spontaneously in gifted beings, to whom abstinence from the grosser indulgences was from temperament easy and almost necessary, others not so constituted endeavoured to induce a similar condition by fasts and mortifications somewhat more painful, because less natural. The former class, when endowed with commanding powers of intellect and an exalted moral nature, occasionally become the master spirits of an epoch. Such seemingly were the founders and great reformers of Brahminism and Budhism, the Avahtars of Vishnu, and the incarnations of Budha ; and such in more historic times was Mahomet. They may be defined as ecstatics of genius. After them generally followed for ages a long train of saints, whose self-imposed penances gave them a degree of illumination more or less approximative to that of their master. Such are the Indian fakirs, the Lamaic recluses, and the Mussulman dervishes. The leaders present us with ecstacy in its highest form, and we might add genius at its maximum, while even among the followers a degree of lucidity is occasionally attained to that few scientifically evoked clairvoyantes have yet reached.

The mystery of such men's power, then, is solved. We call them impostors; their followers knew them to be prophets. We consider their revelations to be the insane ravings of a delirious fanaticism; those who looked at and listened to them were fully persuaded they were "lights from Heaven." It was not those who were most distant from, but those who were nearest to, such mystic moral magnets that most fully felt the force of their resistless attraction. They would bear examination. It was those who had enjoyed the high privilege of talking face to face with the "son of the Koreish," who had seen him hungry, and thirsty, and weary, patching his cloak or mending his sandals—it was these men who formed the vanguard of his saints, the Abdallas or swords of God, who went forth conquering and to conquer in the strength of that inexplicable spirit with which he had so profoundly imbued them. There is a sympathetic atmosphere with which these great spirits are surrounded, and all fitting agents, when once within its range, become the willing satellites of such mighty primaries. If there be any insane raving in this matter, it is on the part of those who, knowing nothing of the nature of such manifestations or visitations, think that an explosion of vulgar abuse or the use of a few hard names will suffice to settle the whole controversy. The rise and growth, the origin and progress of such movements as those we have been alluding to, will never be fully understood, till the essential character of their founders and principal leaders is comprehended. Hitherto they have proved an enigma whereof, however, mesmerism now promises to afford an adequate solution. The rapt visions of lucid meditation, the clear intuition of established errors, and the exalted purpose of a wide-spread and searching reformation are the natural and almost necessary products of the high-wrought enthusiasm of such a being. His interior feeling of vocation to such a mission, his reliance on superhuman support for its accomplishment, and his eloquence so transcendent and resistless in the gifted hour, are all explicable to the experienced mesmerist by his comparative familiarity with approximative conditions in his own subjects. When to this is added the occasional prevision of coming events, the annunciation being subsequently fulfilled, and the frequent revelation of circumstances past or distant that could never be known through the ordinary channels of information, and we have an array of gifts and powers which, although they may now seem merely natural to us, could scarcely fail to impress other generations with an ineradicable idea of the supernatural and the celestial. Shall we sum this matter up, then, by saying that the powers of man which are latent are greater than those which are patent, and that to know the former we must have them revealed under ecstatic exaltation either spontaneous or induced?

One of the grandest truths, indeed, which mesmerism has to unfold to us is this, that the seer is a natural phenomenon and not a preternatural manifestation; that his powers are educed, not communicated; developments from within, not adjuncts from without. But we have seen that these extra-ordinary endowments, which would otherwise apparently have remained dormant, may be evoked into activity in some cases by fasting, devotional exercises, solitude, and other processes calculated to give the mind predominance over the body. By such means self-induced ecstacy may sometimes be obtained, when without them it probably would not manifest itself. But in addition to these phases of mental exaltation there is the lucidity which supervenes by the inhalation of gases, by the application of unguents, and by mesmeric manipulations. The pythia at Delphi are said to have been prepared for their responses by the first, the witches of the middle ages for their dismal saturnalia by the second, and our modern clairvoyantes for their feats of introspection, thought-reading, &c., by the third, which also prevailed, as we have before said, among the Hellenic, Egyptian, and Oriental priesthoods generally.

On few subjects probably are the dissertations of the learned more unsatisfactory than in reference to the important question of oracular responses. In no department of inquiry is their ignorance of the fundamental data, absolutely requisite for the investigation, more apparent. The earlier and more devout, among whom are the fathers, attribute these heathen wonders to the devil; the later and more sceptical are content with the insinuation of trickery and priestcraft. Of these two classes of expositors, the divines certainly exhibited less superficiality than the philosophers; for the former admitted facts too obvious to be denied, and merely advanced an erroneous theory to account for their existence; while the latter in all the pomposity of hypothetical wisdom, have presumed to doubt the testimony of ages, because it witnessed of things for which their theories could furnish no satisfactory explanation. That princes from policy, and the multitude from superstition, should flock to those mystic shrines where truth was oftentimes so enigmatically uttered and futurity so mystically unveiled, was natural; but what shall we say to the fact, that the best and wisest of the philosophers of antiquity also resorted to these fountains of inspiration for additional light on some of the profoundest problems agitated in the schools. Imposture and priestcraft have no doubt done much in the world, but they never yet founded a faith, or originated a world-wide custom. They are the fungi of the old and not the germs of the new, and their presence in any system is one of the surest signs of its decay and approaching dissolution. The pythia were *crisiacs*, wrought up to the requisite point of excitement by processes traditionally handed down among the priesthood of Apollo. Generally selected from among the peasantry of the neighbourhood, they were said to be simple uneducated girls, in no respect competent to their important tasks while in an ordinary condition. Fearfully convulsed while uttering their mystic replies, which were given forth unconsciously as by persons in a state of delirium, they were ignorant on a restoration to their normal condition of all the mighty truths whereof they had been so lately the honoured vehicles. What mesmermist does not here at once recognise the clairvoyant crisis of those early practitioners who, anterior to the time of Puysegur, knew not how to regulate the induction, and generally had a scene of considerable excitement as the accompaniment of a superior manifestation. Ecstatic illumination, then, is the secret spell to which Delphi owed its celebrity and its wealth. This is the fact on which the devotion of ages was founded, the reality on which a graceful polytheism in Greece, and a gloomy idolatry in Egypt, built up that mighty superstructure of sacerdotal power, before which puissant princes bowed their royal necks, and venerable sages became as little children. Let us understand antiquity before we laugh at it. In no age were mankind absolutely fatuous; and the folly of those who deny facts because they cannot understand them is certainly quite equal to that of those who misinterpreted because they did not comprehend them.

LETTER THIRD.

WITCHCRAFT.

WE have in the previous letters contemplated mesmerism as illustrative of ancient seerdom, and that oracular wisdom for which the more celebrated shrines of antiquity were once so illustrious. It was then respectable for it was orthodox. Grandly templed in fanes whose very ruins have been the admiration of all succeeding ages, it had an attendant priesthood eminent for their general learning, and the presumed depositories moreover of mystic truths derived from the remotest past, and incommunicable save to their initiated brethren. Then the person of the pythoness was sacred, and the convulsive throes which indicated the on-coming presence of the god were beheld and spoken of with befitting reverence. Seated on her tripos, and engirdled by her sacerdotal attendants, she saw the wealth of nations placed devoutly at her feet, and found that the fate of kingdoms was supposed to be dependent upon her words. Invocation was then established, and its rights esteemed holy. Apollo was adored as divine, and Isis worshipped as the queen of heaven. But in the resistless cycles of destiny a change was at hand. The flood came which not only overwhelmed Diana of the Ephesians and Minerva of Athens, but at length submerged even the Capitoline and Olympian Jove, with all his subordinate deities, their shrines, and oracles. Christianity arose on the ruins of heathenism, and the deities of the latter sunk into demons, and their once sacred rites into the practice of sorcery. The hierophant became a magician, and the priestess a witch; vaticination was placed among the forbidden arts, and the secrets of the future devoutly committed to the keeping of Satan. He of the triple tira had placed his foot on the neck of antecedent credencies, and incense and holy water were now used, not for the invocation but the expulsion of the diabolic powers of the ante-Christian world.

Of all the melancholy records which render history little else than a chronicle of crimes on the one hand, and of the heroism with which they were resisted on the other, no one is perhaps more truly lamentable than that which narrates the persecution and destruction of witches in the sixteenth and seventeenth centuries. In that scandalous crusade against old women, in which the informers and bloodhounds of the law were urged on both by pecuniary rewards and popular applause, the Church universal stands confessedly guilty. Its clergy of every sect joined in the cry, and the pulpit but too often resounded with those fearful maledictions intended to eventuate in the torture of the feeble, and the death-pangs of the aged. The witch-sermons of this period, indeed, are a disgrace not only to the priesthood who could utter, but to the manhood that could listen to them ; and if either party in this disgraceful mania could be said to be possessed by devils, it was most assuredly the persecutors who inflicted, rather than the persecuted who suffered, such cruel and aggravated injustice. Suffice it, that upon pretences the most frivolous, and on evidence the least conclusive, thousands of helpless women were condemned to a painful and lingering death, generally executed amidst circumstances of insult and shame more terrible to sensitive minds than the direst physical tortures. The fires of the stake consumed the grey hairs of Europe's venerable mothers, who expired amidst the anathemas of the unregenerate and the thanksgivings of the devout. A modern reader of these monstrosities of thought and action would assuredly laugh at their absurdity, were he not too much horrified at their cruelty, and too thoroughly disgusted at their obscenity. Such heartless indifference to human suffering, such dabbling in moral putridity, were certainly never before exhibited in combination, or if so, only in those gloomy chambers where the priests and familiars of the Inquisition put their victims to the question.

So invalid, indeed, was the evidence from without elicited on these witch-trials, that the whole subject might be safely dismissed as unworthy of our attention, except as a fearful instance of the fallibility of human tribunals, and a terrible warning against the excesses of fanaticism, were it not that these external indications, though feeble, are corroborated by internal testimony vastly more convincing. The witches were not merely accused by others of holding unlawful intercourse with Satan, but they frequently confessed to it themselves, and this too on some occasions voluntarily, surrendering themselves to the officers of justice, and demanding to be tried as an expiation for their otherwise unpardonable offences. In many instances, too, confessions rung from these unhappy creatures by the agonizing tortures of their pitiless oppressors were subsequently persevered in even up to the moment of death, the expiring witch dying with the admission of her sin trembling on her lips. Where now, it may be said, is philosophy with its solution, or scepticism with its doubts?

Let us then look at the facts which constituted this well nigh inexpiable sin of witchcraft. What were the supposed acts and what the admitted crimes of these most peccant dames? They anointed themselves with butter, they passed into an insensible trance, they awoke and travelled through the air on a goat or a broomstick, and met on some distant moor or mountain in a vast assemblage, where the devil usually sat as chairman. In addition, they sometimes effected solitary excursions disguised as hares, in which form they were occasionally hunted, and they generally had a resident familiar in the shape of a black cat, their demon in ordinary, and in moments of old-womanish malevolence interfered through his assistance or that of his master with the health of their neighbours' cattle, and occasionally went so far as to touch the very persons of the faithful, on whom they cast divers diseases, and, above all, inducted the devil or some evil spirit into them or their children! Let us translate all this into mesmeric language, and then see how this fanfaronade of superstition reads, clothed in the garb of our new scientific nomenclature. They used a medicated unguent, which being applied simultaneously to the whole surface of the skin, produced such an effect on the nervous system, that a state of insensible coma, was induced, under which, while the corporeal powers were lapped in the somnolent quietude of this abnormal trance, they underwent the subjective experiences of the *sabbat* with its aerial trips and diabolic encounters, the peculiar imagery of their trance-life being derived from the prevalent belief of their age and country, of which it bore the unmistakable impress. Old women at all times have loved cats as young maids do lap-dogs, and the phrenologist finds no difficulty through philoprogenitiveness in accounting for the one or the other, without having resourse to any familiar beyond a quadrupedal succedaneum for an otherwise objectless affection. As to cows rendered milkless and pigs dying of a murrain, it is to be feared that these mishaps do still occur to our agricultural friends, despite the extinction of witches, and, what is of far more importance, a vastly improved method of treating stock. Neither are young ladies yet altogether absolved from the fancies of hysteria, or children quite exculpated from the possessions of epilepsy, albeit medical science has progressed somewhat since the days of the Stuarts. That a poor and despised woman should occasionally look with an envious eye on the possessions of her wealthy neighbour, the substantial yeoman, or that the antiquated virgin or childless widow should behold with a longing gaze the blooming progeny of her junior friends, is not to be wondered at, and needs no especial diabolic prompting to account for its occurrence. That when any of these desirable objects were subsequently smitten by disease or removed by death, the old lady might be accused by others, or, in accordance with the opinions of the time, fancy herself the all-important cause of the disaster, is no more than what our experiences of human nature in all its diversified conditions warrants us in asserting to be not only possible but probable.

But we have as yet by no means exhausted either the facts

or their explanation ; and as the subject is one of considerable importance both historically and philosophically, I shall perhaps be pardoned for entering somewhat more at length into a matter respecting which the benevolent must feel interested, and the curious cannot be readily sated. With the introduction of Christianity, Paganism and its rites fell into desuetude, its temples were deserted, its priesthood neglected, and its ceremonial condemned. Faiths long established, however, are not easily uprooted, and while the newly made converts flocked devoutly to the church, there yet lingered among them for many generations a contraband belief in the objurgated powers of their dethroned heathendom. The deities who had once presided over wood and wild were still feared if not loved, and propitiated as evil spirits if not worshipped as gods. To carry out this forbidden ritual in safest privacy, the lonely glen and barren heath were sought amidst the storms and darkness of the wintry night, and there engirdled with nature in her gloomiest mood, the druids and priests of Odin bequeathed the remnant of their decadent ritual to successors whose qualifications for its effective exercise were ever becoming less and less, and whose education and social position waxed worse with the lapse of every passing age, till at length the majestic organization of Europe's Celtic and Scandinavian hierarchies was represented by the secret and scouted brotherhoods of mediæval magic, while their accomplished priestesses, the haighs and alrunes of other days, appeared in the scarcely recognisable disguise of the witches of the dark ages. Such is a brief historical outline of the origin of those weird sisterhoods, whose ultimate destiny was so fearful to themselves, and such a lasting disgrace to the Christianised civilisation of modern Europe.

That a great majority of the poor creatures who suffered in these dire persecutions were simply ignorant old women, who were either falsely accused by others or fallaciously supposed themselves to be guilty of the sin of witchcraft, we can scarcely doubt. But that so great a movement was based on a nonentity, that the steady belief of mankind through so many successive ages and among so many diversified nations in the existence of extraordinary powers, which could be wielded by an initiated class of mystics, was a baseless fancy, altogether devoid of fact for its foundation, is a supposition untenable on any sound principles of historic criticism. Witchcraft was simply the vulgar and raditionary form of that art, which in its higher phases constituted the magic of ancient and the Rosicrucianism of more recent times. Among scholars and philosophers it would produce such men as Apollonius of Tyana, Cardan, and Paracelsus, whose real powers, magnified and distorted by popular report, formed the basis of those figments under which their science was apprehended by the multitude, and of whose arcane knowledge some fragments were undoubtedly in possession of those lower castes of the learned in occult lore, known as wizards, warlocks, witches, &c. We have seen that some of the latter had the power of producing trance-sleep; under this condition ecstatic lucidity or clairvoyance would in many cases supervene, and of its wonders and supersensuous revelations we have already spoken. They also practically understood what is now known as biology, or in other words the science of impressions, in which they were greatly assisted by the popular belief in and dread of their preternatural powers. Their commands of deprivation were uttered in the form of curses, with which they could strike the sensitive, deaf, dumb, blind, or fatuous, depriving them of all consciousness of their personal identity, and occasionally substituting not only that of another human being, but even that of an animal, as in Lycanthropy or the wolf-disease, under which their wretched victims would howl, bark, or go on all-fours, and rush into the woods in the full persuasion of being turned by a fearful metamorphosis into the form of the creature whose habits they so faithfully imitated. By the same means they could paralyse the limbs and afflict their subjects with all the symptoms of a disease. These impressions they took care not to remove till they had produced their appropriate effect of terror on the spectators and submission on the part of the sufferer; and a few individuals being thus primarily affected, would soon by sympathy, affect others, till at length such morbid symptoms would become epidemic, and rage over whole districts like a nervous plague, propagated on the same principle as the excitement of the Flagellants or the dancing mania of the Jumpers. In many instances the mere fancy of the victims was enough; the witch had no need of defining the exact form under which her maleficent desires should be manifested; a look full of hate, a muttered curse of unutterable meaning, sufficed; the arrow had sped home, and all that a depressed or agitated mind could accomplish was in due time effected, till strong men drooped in their prime, and blooming maidens pined like flowers stricken in the bud.

The remedy for all this is, I need scarcely say, not cruelty but knowledge. That which eventually stayed these terrors was not the burning of witches, but the advancing education of the people; and the most effective preventative to their recurrence under any other form is not the ignorant maledictions of the theologian, but the scientific explanation of the philosopher. It was the supposition that the power which they exercised was preternatural that gave these beldames their tremendous ability for mischief. An exposition of its essential character would have proved the destruction of their influence, for they lived in and on the popular delusion by which they were evoked and sustained. But while popes issued bulls, and kings composed volumes on the sin of witchcraft, in the full persuasion of its being a thoroughly supernatural affair, it is no wonder that the masses were misled. The evil indeed was fearfully aggravated by the very means used to prevent it, for clerical zeal and judicial gravity, eventuating in the murderous duties of the executioner, sealed and stamped by the death of thousands the reality and truthfulness of that popular misapprehension, which a more enlarged science would have dispelled, and a more enlightened philosophy might have rectified.

LETTER FOURTH.

EXORCISM, MAGIC, AND ENCHANTMENT.

HAVING in a previous letter contemplated what may be termed the vulgar, I now purpose more especially developing the learned aspect of mediæval superstition, in its connection with misapprehended mesmeric phenomena. We have seen that witches were supposed to occasionally induct the devil, or one of his assistants, into the body of some unfortunate; of course the most appropriate remedy in such a case was the ejection of this intruder by a priest, the good Father's Latin being supposed, perhaps not without some show of reason, too much even for such an auditor. Of these extraordinary proceedings, fortunately for science, many detailed narrations remain, in which the symptoms of the possessed patient, and the processes of his sacerdotal physician, are narrated with all that minuteness and care which the gravity of the occasion seemed to demand. There is an earnest faith, too, in the historians of these strange occurrences, which is not the least interesting portion of the affair, more especially to a modern, whose risibility is generally excited by the ludicrous, precisely at the point where the antiquated annalist intended him to be most profoundly affected by the terrible. Occasionally indeed, these diabolic encounters partake so largely of the comic, that we are almost tempted to think the chroniclers of the period must have indulged at times in a vein of delicate irony on their clerical contemporaries, the battery being masked under the pretence of recounting some wonderful victory achieved over tne powers of darkness, lodged for the time in that rather dilapidated citadel, the body of some half-witted maniac or convulsed epileptic. In

not a few instances, however, the belligerent clergyman becomes, of course with all due humility, the historian of his
own conflicts with the infernal "principalities and powers,"
in which case we are generally furnished with a most graphic
and gratifying description of the warfare in all its successive
stages of development, from the first challenge of the
Churchman and the defiant answer of the fiend, up to
the final retreat of the latter, thoroughly confounded and
overcome by a torrent of Latin, Greek, and Hebrew,
and making his exit in utter discomfiture under "the
rogue's march," executed in full choir from the "drums
ecclesiastic."

There seems, indeed, to be a stage of civilization, or rather
of barbarism, at which diseases are generally attributed not
to physical but spiritual agencies, and as curses rather than
blessings they are very naturally assigned to the influence of
maleficent more than beneficent beings.   Some such idea is
prevalent at present among the Indians of America, the
negroes of Africa, and the nomadic hordes of Eastern Asia.
Among the latter, indeed, it would appear that demons of such
dignity sometimes make their appearance, that not only one
horse but many fully caparisoned are demanded by the learned
exorcist, a Lamaic priest, to carry this infernal dignitary and
his attendants fairly off the field.   It need scarcely be said
that fiends of such rank never condescend to molest any but
wealthy patients, there being, it seems, a sort of co-ordination
established between the diseased and their tormentors, so that
a poor man has at least the satisfaction of knowing that no
very potent prince of darkness is likely to afflict him with any
of those preternatural ills to which these Budhistic Tartars
seem more than usually liable.   Through this rather transparent veil the petty cunning and grasping avarice of a rude
though powerful hierarchy are no doubt sufficiently apparent.
But let us remember our former canon of criticism.   Priests do
not originate but only profit by popular superstition.   The
clergy of Europe did but inherit and sustain the ideas of their
time in reference to possession, witchcraft, &c., in the reality

of which some of them had doubtless as profound a belief as the least enlightened of the laity.

What then, it may be asked, were the demoniacs of our mediæval annalists, and what relationship did their exorcists hold to these pitiable creatures? The former were maniacs, epileptics, or spontaneous crisiacs, and the latter were unconsciously their mental mesmerists. The accession of the disease was accounted the incession of the demon, and the symptoms of a crisis were esteemed the effects of his special fury. The ordinary contortions, foamings, and howlings which were usually manifested at certain stages of this morbus sacer, are simply the symptoms of a paroxysm of epilepsy. But in addition to this, we are told the possessed sometimes became perfectly rigid, and quite insensible, at other times they would exhibit a degree of strength or agility to which in their ordinary condition they could not even approximate. But these corporeal displays were the most insignificant part of the peculiarities attendant on this deplorable condition. These unfortunates, although ignorant, would occasionally speak with astonishing volubility on the most abtruse topics, and when addressed in Latin or even Greek, would reply in their own language, with an obvious comprehension of the full meaning of their learned interlocutor. Nay, so witty and eloquent would even dull peasants become when thus exalted by infernal inspiration, that they not unfrequently put even the most accomplished clergymen to shame, who but for a praiseworthy zeal in their holy vocation, would sometimes have been absolutely silenced by the eloquent impertinence of the intrusive demon. Nor was this all, for in many instances the spirit, speaking through the miserable subject, is said to have revealed the secret thoughts or past actions of the exorcist or bystanders—to have replied to questions put mentally, and occasionally to have truly foretold impending occurrences. While not least among the wonderful features of this distressing malady, was the fact of general unconsciousness on the part of the patient in his ordinary condition of all the horrors thus transacted while more immediately under the influence of possession. Our good forefathers no doubt thought that these were indications enough of the presence of unsanctified influences. We, however, have no difficulty here in recognising all the symptoms of a clairvoyant or ecstatic crisis, somewhat disturbed in its manifestation by the ignorance of the exorcist, and greatly aggravated by the belief, both of the subject and his friends, that the affair was a supernatural visitation instead of a natural disease. The exorcist when endowed with a strong will and great nervous energy frequently cured his patient, or, in the language of the time, expelled the demon ; but when the weaker of the two, or deficient in courage or faith, he sometimes became the victim of his rashness, and in not a few cases we find that the operator so far sympathised with his subject as to become himself affected with the very disease of which he was attempting to relieve another. In the celebrated case of the nuns of Loudun, it was observed that all who exorcised these unfortunate ladies were in turn attacked by the malady which they endeavoured to cure. The experienced mesmerist has here no difficulty in recognising the effects of sympathetic reaction from a powerful subject on a comparatively weak and inefficient operator. Such were the exorcism and possession of the middle ages. A scientific mistake rather than a clerical imposition ; an error not a crime ; the fruit not of intentional deception but popular ignorance ; a delusion not as to the facts, which were real, but as to their causes and essential character, which were misapprehended.

Let us now conclude this survey of ancient mesmerism under its superstitious aspect by a few remarks on magic, not the natural and mechanical, but the preternatural and psychical To this class of phenomena belong those tales of invulnerability and invisibility with which the old narrations of sorcery so frequently abound. These highly valuable qualities attached to the magician, only in relation to those under his influence, within his sphere, in modern phrase, to his subjects. Now, whoever has seen a good biologist operate, will be at no loss to understand how the most substantial sorcerer might remain intact and unseen by any number of his surrounding disciples, although in the very midst of them. Feasts called up by the wand of an enchanter, money which turned to nothing in the hands of those to whom it was paid, and even gardens and palaces evoked in the barren wilderness, at the word of command, are now easily explicable; they were impressions on the mind, not the senses of the percipients. So the wondrous metamorphosis of either the magician or his subjects into animals, trees, or furniture, were phenomena of a subjective not objective character. From the prevalence of tales similar to the foregoing, it would seem that the art of impressing a large number of persons simultaneously must have been better understood by the mediæval thaumauturgists than by their modern successors; for after every allowance for exaggeration in the narration, it would seem that their operations in the way of enchantment were certainly upon a larger scale and with less of preparation, than would be possible with our present knowledge.

It has been customary to account for the wonderful visions and fearful experiences of those who were initiated into the ancient mysteries both in Greece and Egypt, by attributing all the appearances to machinery, Heaven and Hell, Elysium and Tartarus, with their respective occupants, being supposed to be revealed simply by artistic contrivances for stage effect. Something, no donbt, was due to this, but the fasts and purifications all indicate a preparation for mesmeric rather than mechanical impressions, and psychic rather than sensuous experiences. Moreover, as processes derived from the East, and in which sanctity and secrecy combined to maintain the primeval forms and traditions unaltered from generation to generation, we have strong corroborative evidence of the presence of something more serious and awe-inspiring than the vulgar tricks of scene-shifting, artificial perspective, ventriloquism, and legerdemain. The old man of the mountain, the father of the assassins at the time of the crusades, knew better, and impressed his devoted followers, not by clumsy contrivances to impose on the senses, but by powerful instrumentalities for evoking and acting on the tremendous susceptibilities of the trance-life. Historians have yet much to learn, and high as antiquity may now be esteemed for its known wisdom, it has yet to stand much higher with posterity for that which is at present unknown. Its lost lore was obviously of a much profounder character than that which has been preserved, so that it is only when guided by the latest discoveries of modern science that we are enabled to gather up and understand even the fragmentary remnants of its once grand system of occult knowledge, the indications of which were useless to our predecessors from their ignorance of the phenomena referred to, and which are doubtless susceptible of but a partial interpretation even from ourselves.

LETTER FIFTH.

DREAMS.

HAVING in the previous letters contemplated mesmerism in connection with ancient superstition, it now only remains, by way of completing our survey of this department of the science, to notice its presence as a source of certain recondite phenomena, on which in virtue of their apparently mysterious and inexplicable character, a considerable amount of popular mis-apprehension still prevails. We flatter ourselves, or rather we are flattered by certain literary and scientific gentlemen, the leaders of public opinion, into the belief that in this western portion of Europe mankind have altogether out-grown the influence of supernaturalism. This is the established creed of all respectable periodicals, daily, weekly, monthly, and quarterly, or rather it was their creed, for of the effectual eradication of this noxious weed of superstition some grave doubts seem of late to be entertained even by the most confi-dent advocates of human progress. That it was ever more than superficially covered up and hedged round by the ban of fashionable society, everybody who had travelled beyond the carpeted proprieties of a drawing-room or emerged from the book-shelf artificialities of the library, knew right well. The people never were free from its influence, while the ex-travagant zeal with which every seeming novelty of the occult order is sought out and patronised even by the most select and exclusive, may suffice to show to the least observant how powerful is this tendency of our nature, even in minds the most carefully disciplined to resist its influence. What with celestial telegraphs in Paris, spirit rappings in America, and crystal divinations and fashionable astrology in " the west or worst end of a certain city," we have had ample evidence of late that the smouldering embers of a seemingly quiescent spiritualism, may any day be blown into a most respectable blaze, provided only that appropriate influences can be set in motion. Let preternaturalism come cloaked in the garb of science, that is, in the mental costume of the nineteenth century, and it will not only be at once and unhesitatingly received by vast multitudes, even of the highly educated, but will stand as fair a chance now of creating a mania, as any witchcraft, devilry, or vampyrism of other ages.

But in addition to, or rather underlying these more temporary and evanescent manifestations of excitement, we find still surviving amidst the debris of many antiquated forms of heterodox faith a considerable amount of popular belief in the presence and power of agents, not only invisible and intangible, but also supposed to be beyond the bounds of nature and without the domain of her rigidly fixed and immutable laws. Such are ghosts, wraiths, and all the attendant phenomena of haunted houses or places; while second sight, prophetic dreams, presentiments, and other aspects of pre - vision, suffice to show that a lingering belief in the gifts of vaticination, still slumbers uneasily in the profounder depths of consciousness, biding its time for a second and terrible awakening.

The glory of dream-land has departed, or rather has passed from the throne to the footstool, from the prince to the peasant, from the palace to the cottage. Once it was customary for monarchs to consult their pillows as well as their ministers, and not unfrequently did they prefer the indications of the former to the advice of the latter. Armies were marched or halted, and decrees issued or suspended, according to the nocturnal presentments of somnolent majesty. The king's sleep, and we may thence presume his digestion also, was once indeed a state affair of no little moment; for upon these important items often depended the coming in or going out of Grand Viziers, and the appointment or recal of those primitive pachas, the mighty satraps of the ancient oriental monarchies. We have a specimen of this in the ex-

periences of the Babylonian Nebuchadnezzar; and when we
consider that there was not always a Daniel to come to judgment, it must be obvious that no little incertitude thence
resulted to all the parties most nearly concerned. The influence of the royal bed-chamber, indeed must have proved
almost as constant a source of vexation and anxiety to faithful
ministers and statesmen then, as certain chambers of the representative order do now in those inconvenient establish-
ments, the constitutional monarchies of modern Europe. Were
the men of those early generations, then, fools to believe in
a lie, and permit both their public and private affairs to be
regulated by a set of cunning priests and grave impostors,
who, under the pretence of interpreting the nocturnal fancies
of a nightmare dream, contrived to pull the wires by which
state puppets, with crowns or without them, danced at their
bidding? We rather think not; although this is doubtless the
charitable interpretation which thousands of worldly-wise
philosophers have put upon the whole matter.

What, then, is the fact? On what natural phenomenon was
this tremendous superstructure reared, in which so many
generations of magian interpreters found comfortable lodg-
ment, and whence, as from a masked battery, so many able
statesmen and puissant commanders were forced to retreat in
hopeless discomfiture? On the fact that a state of ecstasy is
frequently accompanied by the development of pre-vision and
supersensuous perception; and on the additional fact, that
natural sleep may by art be converted into the mesmeric, and
may also, where there is a constitutional predisposition to the
trance-life, be so converted without art, the nervous system
being in such cases generally acted on either by indisposition
or the excitement which accompanies intense thought or
anxiety. The visions of ecstatic slumber, in short, may be
endowed with all the peculiarities usually attendant on the
mental operations of a clairvoyant subject. Hence the dreams
of a lucide or natural seer, may be prophetic or retrospective,
and afford revelations of distant or secret circumstances. It
is the rarity and not the impossibility of such a phenomenon

which renders the attention to ordinary dreaming as a guide in the affairs of life so grievous an absurdity. Of the occasional devolopment of such a power, however, even in our own day, no reasonable doubt can be entertained by those who have taken the trouble to carefully investigate the data afforded by well-authenticated narrations of "remarkable dreams," as they are usually called, that is, of nocturnal visions subsequently found to be susceptible of verification. The comparative simplicity of primeval life, the rapt spirituality of patriarchal devotion, and the few but grand and sublime ideas which constituted their subject-matter of meditation to the earlier generations of mankind, were all eminently favourable to the development of that ecstatic crisis which constituted the waking or dreaming seer, as it occured in the vigilant or somnolent condition of the system.

The foregoing remarks apply to dream revelations, which were direct, the imagery being a transcript of the outward event, and to unravel the mystery of which consequently no interpreter was needed. But it seems there was another class of the analogical order, in which physical objects were supposed to represent complex ideas, trees, mountains, &c., meaning empires, principalities, powers, and systems. This was the favourite sphere of the magian priesthood, who were professionally devoted to the translation of this hieroglyphical language into the common tongue. Men's belief in dream lore commenced with the former, resting on the sure but simple basis of reality, but it perished amidst the mystic pretensions and high sounding fallacies of the latter, which drew on human credulity till, in the reaction of an indignant scepticism, the facts of nature were for the time buried and forgotten amidst the neglected debris of detected trickery and antiquated imposture. Of the essential distinction between lucid dreams and the chaotic presentments of ordinary sleep, however, some of the classic ancients seem to have been fully aware, and typified this under the figure of the ivory and horny gate; the visions which came through the one being reliable, while those which arrived through the other were fallacious.

In addition to these dreams of a prophetic there are others of a retrospective character, in which however a clairvoyant power is nevertheless obviously developed. An instance of this was narrated in the papers some years since, and made a considerable impression at the time, in consequence of its connection with a celebrated murder case then attracting that morbid attention usually bestowed on such horrors. A young woman named Maria Martin had quitted her mother's cottage one evening with the purpose, it was supposed, of taking a short walk; but she never returned. Inquiry after the living absentee and search for her body proved alike ineffectual. Her mother, however, after the lapse of a few weeks, dreamed that her missing daughter had been murdered, and buried beneath the floor of a building known as the red barn. This dream was repeated, and left such an impression on the old woman's mind that she not only spoke of it to her poorer neighbours, but eventually, by importunity, succeeded in interesting the clergyman of the parish and some other influential parties, who, rather to satisfy the pardonable fancies of the bereaved mother than with any faith in the success of their undertaking, permitted the barn to be examined, and there, a few feet beneath the surface, they found the remains of the unfortunate girl. Eventually evidence was obtained from other sources, which produced the conviction of Caudor, a farmer's son of the neighbourhood, who prior to the execution confessed his guilt. The savans of course declared this was an extraordinary coincidence, and so shelved the inconvenient because inexplicable fact of a perfect congruity between the dream and reality. The educated public wondered, and the vulgar believed and reverenced. All were a little mystified; but after a time this, like many similar instances of somnolent revelation, was carelessly committed to that oblivion in which data not in accordance with a dominant philosophy are so conveniently lost.

Now, what is the real explanation of this seeming wonder? The mother living in the comparative solitude of a rural district, was doubtless a woman of but few ideas; the mys-

terious disappearance of her daughter thus occupied and overspread her whole being, she thought and felt about little else
day after day. Such fixity of attention, combined as it usually
is with grief or any other all absorbing passion, is eminently
favourable to the production of ecstacy—is the process, in
short, by which self-induced or spontaneous lucidity has been
in all ages produced. In this case maternal love, wounded
by deprivation of its object under circumstances especially
productive of anxiety, evoked the latent susceptibility of the
old peasant into manifestation, but in the somnolent, not the
vigilant form. She became a lucid dreamer, and penetrated
the veil behind which an apparently successful assassin had
secreted the condemning evidence of his villany. It is also
possible that a *rapport* might have been established between
her mind and that of the murderer, whose agitated and self-
accusing thoughts would no doubt often turn to the simple
cottage and the aged parents, whence and from whom he had
lured the devoted and confiding girl, not merely to her ruin
but her death. The foregoing narrative and its explanation
will of course suffice as an illustration of the workings of those
profounder laws of our being, in other and similar instances,
on which a superficial science has long looked with supercilious contempt, but to which a profounder wisdom is now
directing its most earnest attention.

Besides these revelations of actual fact, there are some
dreams which may be termed sympathetic, where two persons
simultaneously but without previous consent either experience
the same dream or perform their respective parts in one scene,
existing with all its accessories only in the nocturnal cloud-
land of the two constantaneous minds. Cases of this kind
have occurred where letters detailing the impressive experiences of each person have crossed on the road, and been
contemporaneously received to the no small astonishment of all
the parties concerned. A case of this kind is narrated by Dr
Abercrombie in his work on the " Intellectual Powers," and
similar phenomena are spoken of by the German writers as
occurring not unfrequently in fatherland. The mesmeric fact

of community of thought and feeling between an operator and his subject, will at once illustrate and explain this seemingly mysterious circumstance.

Enough has, however, I trust, now been said to show the importance of this portion of our complex being to the metaphysician, and to commend it to the notice of all who would investigate and understand something more of the mystery of our inner existence, than is revealed in those stock works on moral philosophy, with which the reading world has been inundated for the last century. Dreams, like other rather occult phenomena, have been subjected at successive periods to the contrasted fate of a superstitious reverence which declared investigation to be impious, and a philosophic indifference that esteemed it needless. Thus condemned to obscurity both by the fear of the ignorant and the neglect of the learned, this most interesting department of inquiry has been hitherto overlooked Its time for receiving due but enlightened attention has, however, now arrived, and it will soon be acknowledged that, until we comprehend the somnolent as well as the vigilant operations of the human mind, our views in reference to it must of necessity be partial, and our ideas consequently erroneous.

LETTER SIXTH.

SECOND SIGHT AND PRESENTIMENTS.

THE observations contained in my previous letter on dreams, in which a supersenuous exaltation of the faculties has been approximately attained to, combined with the illustrations contained in Letter Second on the essential character of seerdom, will doubtless have prepared the reader's mind for the following explanation of second sight, a gift by no means confined to the Scottish Highlands, although manifested at one time among the mountaineers of Caledonia in a very high degree of development, and in more than ordinary frequency. Obscured amidst the artificiality of a complex civilization, extinguished alike by the drudgery of divided labour, and the deadening routine of scholastic studies, the intuitions of the inner life of contemplation are now generally overlaid and beclouded by the daily demands of our outer life of action and acquisition. Man at present occupied with commerce, politics, literature, and science, projects himself with such force upon the objective sphere that he has neither inclination nor ability for a descent into the profounder depths of the subjective. He lives in the world without so constantly that he is a stranger to the still grander world within. Bnt amidst the vast solitudes of the eastern desert, and in the sublime loneliness of their Alpine homes, the prophets and seers both of the East and West have at various periods cultured those psychic capabilities, in proportion to whose growth and expansion light wells up from those mystic recesses of our being, whose fountains are sealed to all but the gifted idealists, who dwell in the indescribable radiance of interior illumination. Stamped with the characteristics of their race, the specialities

of their faith, and the idiosyncracy of their several individual-
ities, the visions of these seers might be conversant about the
transmigrations of Indian theosophy, the houris of a Mahom-
medan paradise, the immortal war-feasts of Odin, or the
simplest details of their own, their neighbours' or their chief-
tains' fortunes. It was under the latter or social aspect
that this endowment was generally manifested by the High-
landers and Islanders of Scotland, their revelations having
reference generally to the details of social life, deaths, mar-
riages, " accidents by flood and field," and more rarely to
impending or distant military movements.

In accordance with the sceptical but shallow philosophy of
the last few generations, it has been customary to doubt and
laugh at the pretensions of our Celtic prophets, which were but
too obviously beyond the circuit of existing science.   Hence
to believe became unfashionable, for with all its professions of
respect for the memory of Francis of Verulam, modern philosophy finds no difficulty in eschewing facts for whose existence
no plausible hypothesis can be framed.   Lucidity was not
within its category of acknowledged phenomena, and hence
results dependent for their manifestation upon its presence
were systematically ignored.   Second sight was unanimously
voted a superstition, and all the records of its existence placed
in the *index expurgatorius* of those enlightened schools which
professed to receive the *Novum Organum* as a guide and
nature as an authority !   A change, however, has been coming
over the spirit of our dreams within the last few years, and in
the reaction against a gross and purely materialistic scepticism,
there is some danger of running into the opposite extreme of a
rampant spiritualism.   Fortunately a profounder philosophy
and a more expansive science have at length been evolved, and
we can now contemplate the tales of superstition with that
enlightened self-possession, which is neither alarmed by the
groundless terrors of the ignorant nor repelled by the superficial
scepticism of the partially learned.   We are willing to receive
the facts of second sight, not on their probability, that is, their
congruity, or otherwise with our preconceived ideas, but on

their evidence, that is, the amount and character of the testimony which may be producible as to the actual manifestation of such a faculty.

What, then, it may be asked, is second sight? To what order of phenomena is it most nearly related, and on what laws of nature does it depend for its manifestation? It is a species of waking and conscious clairvoyance, and is allied to all those forms of ecstatic lucidity or interior illumination of which I have already spoken, as dependent on mesmeric manipulation, or as of spontaneous development among the seers of various ages and countries. It is the exhibition of a faculty which, usually latent, can nevertheless be evoked in certain instances by the use of appropriate agencies, and in other cases becomes spontaneously active, either from constitutional predisposition or the stimulation afforded by intense or long-continued mental excitement. It is sometimes communicable by contact, it is said, even to individuals not so gifted, as when a seer in a state of vision touches a person not at the time so affected, when the latter frequently partakes of the exaltation, and thus becomes sympathetically percipient of objects to whose presence though antecedently insensible, he has been rendered susceptible by interspheration with the primal seer. This is an instance of that community of thought and feeling with which the higher range of mesmeric experiments have now rendered us comparatively familiar. This process, however, would seem to be productive but of a temporary result, the faculty of seer-vision either ceasing immediately on the breach of contact, or at the farthest not lasting beyond this one presentment of the vision-sphere. But another and more effective procedure was occasionally resorted to for the permanent communication of seer power. In this case the individual desirous of receiving the afflatus, placed himself on his back at full length on the ground, his arms being extended with the palms of the hands uppermost. The seer then lay upon him, hand to hand, and foot to foot, and breathed over his face, and it is said into his mouth, nostrils, and ears, repeating at the same time some traditional charm. A more powerful process of mesmerisation could scarcely be conceived of; its essential character cannot be mistaken; and there is no doubt that with a duly susceptible patient it has often proved successful. The lucid crisis was also sometimes purposely evoked, when specially wanted for any particular occasion, by absorption into the system of the finer properties of animal life, as in the instance so beautifully described by Sir Walter Scott, in the 4th canto of "The Lady of the Lake," where Brian, the seer of Roderick Dhu, wraps himself in the raw and reeking hide of a recently slain bull, and thus obtains those prophetic revelations which were to direct his chieftain's future movements. This, I may remark, was one of the inducements to ancient vaticinatory sacrifice, both human and bestial, namely, the supposed connection of this awful rite with the mystic induction of lucidity in the sacrificer. Divination by the entrails was the exoteric, but the sympathetic communication thus supposed to be established with the occult essences of things, was the esotoric doctrine of the ancient sacerdotal slaughtermen. In addition to this use of the raw hide of a sacrificed animal as a coverlid, the seer sometimes adopted the process of gazing fixedly on a star, a sublime act of self-mesmerisation, and one too, which opens up a new view of the real powers once attributed by the ancient astrologers to the heavenly bodies.

Such, then, is second sight, the social seerdom of the West, the lowly germ of a mighty power, which, in the master spirits of Brahminism, Budhism, and Mahomedanism, has founded faiths which have flourished in power for ages, and whose lingering remnants still present a most formidable barrier to the diffusion of European ideas and the establishment of Christianised institutions in the East. To overlook the existence of such a power, as an ever-present though usually latent capability in man, is to misunderstand and ignore one of the most important attributes of humanity. To disregard the presence and influence of such an endowment as one of the motive or rather plastic forces of human destiny, is to exclude from our investigation of the past and our esti-

mate of the probabilities of the future, one of the most pow·
erful and lasting agencies which has ever effected a fundamental change in the faith, and through it in the character
and destiny of nations. Ecstatics, that is, seers or second sight
men, be it remembered, have been the prophets, legislators,
and sages of antecedent times, and as such have exerted a
power over the minds of their followers, which, for depth,
extent, and duration, laughs to scorn the utmost influence
ever claimed for the prevalent literature and philosophy of our
day. They were men whose shadow still covers the Eastern
world—whose names are repeated in the daily devotions of
hundreds of millions of our fellow beings as a pass-word to the
throne of Omnipotence, and upon the authority of whose precepts and the force of whose example, the thoughts and
actions of generation after generation are still sedulously and
reverentially formed. Such they were in the past. Let
Mormonism, that faint shadow of things to come, teach what
with due excitement and fitting opportunity they may,
humanly speaking, yet accomplish in the future.

Dreams and second sight, however, whether true or false,
celestial revelations or chaotic shadows, are for the vulgar and
the ignorant, and to speak of such things to ears polite would,
it is to be feared, only excite a very grave suspicion of one's
own aural appendages being more distinguished by longitude
than is esteemed compatible with unshaded clearness of
comprehension. Custom has not only expelled them from the
court, but has excluded them from the drawing-room; and
but for the obscure refuge afforded by the kitchen and the
cottage, dream-land might have been a realm no longer recognised as existent in European society. But it is quite
otherwise with a certain allied sphere of the occult and pre-
dictive. I allude to presentiments. These are still heroic
and regal, for conquerors and crowned heads may occasionally
profess to have thus received some faint intimation, to have
had some dim apprehension of coming events, which are
poetically said to cast their shadows before, and yet, by such
profession, suffer no diminution of victor-glory or imperial

dignity. It is not weak but strong minds, not the mill-horse regulars of thought and action, ever treading the same dull round of motionless activity, but the knight-errant adventurers of Dame Fortune, with their varied experiences and profoundly evocative excitement, who are generally the most susceptible to influences of this class. The boundless aspirations of an Alexander, the unwavering ambition of a Cæsar, the dauntless courage of a Cromwell, and the grasping genius of a Napoleon, were all perfectly compatible with the entertainment of such a weakness; while the reforming zeal and fearless energy of a Luther, and the ardent piety and exhaustless assiduity of a Wesley, were no safeguards against the inroads of this subtle superstition, which still prevails, indeed openly or secretly, in the court and the camp, unextinguished amidst the wordy warfare of senatorial conflict, and still surviving in those manly bosoms whose lion hearts have been tried amidst the howlings of the midnight tempest, and trained under the thunder of that artillery, whose bolts bear death and carnage from those floating citadels to which Britain owes at once her safety and her power.

What, then, is a presentiment? Does it rest on the firm foundations of fact, or is it a mere figment of the imagination? Are these dim promonitions referable to fixed laws and ascertained forces, or are they but the confused shadows of a distempered fancy? Can science throw any light on this strange phenomenon, or must it be left as an insoluble problem amongst those inscrutable mysteries which ever hedge our life in time? A presentiment may be defined as an imperfectly apprehended prophesy; it is an enunciation through the feelings rather than the intellect, an instinctive anticipation rather than a precalculated expectancy. It is, in short, the foreshadowment of a dim and imperfectly developed clairvoy-ance, and may be derived either from the faint traceries of a lucid dream, subsequently almost forgotten, or from an ap-proximation more or less remote to the state of vigilant ecstacy. The rule with mesmeric subjects is oblivion on a return to consciousness of all the varied experiences of the trance-life; and who shall say but a similar law prevails in reference to the somnolent revelations of spontaneous lucidity when obtained during sleep. All that would then remain of a foreseen event would be a vague impression on the mind of impending good or evil, in connection with some person, place, time, or circumstance, this feeling becoming more and more powerful as, with an approximation to the grand result, and the actual occurrence of antecedent but previsioned accessories, the law of association would suffice to recall the shadowy outlines of the greater event with which they stood connected in the forgotten dream. Thus reminiscence would be partially awakened, and the evanescent impressions of trance-life so far recalled as to permit of the production of those feelings which we know as presentiments, the latter being vague or definite in proportion to the degree in which the dream vision whence they originated was recollected or lost. Such is probably the origin of one class of presentient impressions, with which also another mental phenomenon seems to be nearly connected; I allude to the mysterious feeling with which some persons are said to be affected, who on a first interview with a stranger, or at their first visit to a place, have, notwithstanding their vivid consciousness of its absurdity, an inexplicable yet irresistible feeling of having passed through the same experiences before; but when, or where, or how, they are incapable of explaining. An antecedent dream of the clairvoyant order, forgotten till revealed by the recurrence in the objective sphere of that which had been previously undergone in the subjective, would afford an easy solution of this seemingly inscrutable peculiarity. Another class of presentiments seem, as we have said to arise from an imperfect development of the clairvoyant faculty in the waking state. The lucidity is incomplete, and consequently affords but occasional and imperfect glimpses of the yet untrodden realm of the future, and hence like the imperfectly remembered dream, is manifested rather in the vagueness of a feeling than the definitiveness of an idea.

Such are the facts, and such we may say is the philosophy,

of that faint and evanescent form of seerdom which has survived to our day, triumphing as by the tenacity of an inex-
tinguishable life over the hard scepticism and cold calculation
of our nineteenth century. The mysterious presentiment
seems invincible; on those who are affected by it ridicule is
lost, and before their ineradicable convictions the keenest wit
is powerless. They let society laugh but they retain their
opinions. They can listen while the logician shows the absurdity of their feelings, but they have a ground of faith which
he knows not of, a well-spring within, whose light trans-
cends that of the clearest demonstration. Dialectics indeed
will ever fail before inspiration, and even the force of induction is lost on one whose psychic experience belies the truth
which objective facts would teach him. The weight of a
presentiment is known by internal evidence, and can be ap-
preciated only by those gifted or troubled with such an interior
illumination. Practically I would not advise those favoured
or annoyed by such intuitions to act needlessly in opposition
to their internal, shall we say their better monitor.

" We are wiser than we know ;"

and these instinctive promptings seem to be given to some
natures as a necessary complement to percipient and reflective
faculties, not perhaps in every case quite competent to the
guidance of their possessor through all the manifold intricacies
and unforeseeable casualties of a life more than ordinarily
productive of mortal dangers and trying emergencies.

LETTER SEVENTH.

VILLAGE GHOSTS AND FAIRIES.

AMONG the many other notable things which modern philosophy prides itself upon having converted from a palpable solid into the most evanescent of all aeriform bodies, from the sternest of realities into the purest of idealisms, we may decidedly enumerate ghosts. They have been exploded, declared in all councils of *savans* to be nonentities, and any, even the faintest shadow of belief in their existence pronounced upon the highest authority, heterodox. To allude to them seriously in good society would be esteemed simply a mark of ill-breeding, for they have been long since rigidly excluded from all select circles. Poor ghosts, what a change of fortune since the time when they were esteemed befitting associates for royalty, and could regularly visit the palatial halls and regal tents of the Macbeths and Richards of other times. Like many shining and fashionable characters, these spiritual visitants, it seems, have had their day, and considering over how many centuries it lasted, they certainly have little to complain of in reference to its length. Nevertheless, ghosts are a humanitarian tradition; they have apparently troubled men in all ages, and made themselves duly presentible in every stage of civilization, and under every form of faith. Job the patriarch, and Brutus the Roman, alike professed to have seen them; and if philosophers, the men of matter, have occasionally doubted, poets, the men of soul, have almost universally believed in, and, we may remark, used them. They must be esteemed vulgar now, but there was a time when no ancient family would have conceived its hereditary honours to be duly supported without a regular household attendant of the spiritual order, for the dignified announcement of impending death and misfortune. White ladies and shrieking women, indeed, were once considered the necessary appendages of a lordly or regal mansion, devoid of which it lacked something of the importance that a due recognition of its existence on the part of the supernal powers could alone confer. In point of geographical extent it is also obvious that the influence of ghosts must be considered as truly mundane, for while the negro fears their presence in the dense forests and tangled underwood of the Torrid Zone, the Laplander equally dreads their apparition amidst the gloom of those wintry nights that girdle his polar home with months of darkness. The Tartar shepherd of the East, and the agricultural peasant of the West, are alike the victims of this widely-spread superstition, which also has its devotees in the heart of Europe's mighty capitals and on the thinly peopled prairies, where the American hunter tracks the elk and buffalo over the majestic wilds of primeval and unsubdued nature. A faith so long enduring and so extensively diffused must, on all our previously admitted principles of investigation, be esteemed as something more than a mere delusion—must be considered as the embodiment of a great fact, thus emphatically declared by so many witnesses to have an actual existence. Let us then examine the subject somewhat more closely, and endeavour, if possible, to discover the small substratum of reality, whose magnified shadow has thus overspread so many ages and countries.

That there are now and have at all times been many ghost seers, that is, veracious persons who profess to have seen the spirits of their departed friends or of strangers unknown to them, cannot for a moment be doubted by those at all acquainted with the literature of other ages, or with the real opinions and feelings of mankind at present. The ridicule of the wit and the reasoning of the philosopher may drive these things beneath the surface; but go forth into real society, emerge from the "cabined, cribbed, confined" ideas of a few artificially cultured coteries—be the trusted friend and familiar guest of families not simply of one but many classes—be received into the homes and the confidence of households in town and country. and in province after province—and you will know that here, in these British islands, and in the middle of this nineteenth century, ghosts are still spoken of by thousands as awful realities and terrible presences, to doubt and deny whose visitations would imply, not knowledge but ignorance. Much of the fashionable scepticism indeed now professed in reference to spiritual appearances is a mere cuckoo cry, kept up by imitation and reiterated by those who have never had an opportunity of investigating the matter by conversation with the actual seers. The prevalent opinions on this subject are in truth but the echo of our dominant philosophy, whose rationalistic principles are the procustean bed to which all facts must be shaped or pronounced inadmissable. Ghosts are of course very inconvenient to those who think that mathematics and mechanism can settle everything, and that chemistry and optics will afford a solution for every presentment which has come within the limits of human experience. A change, however, in relation to this, as well as many other correlated departments of inquiry, has now obviously commenced, and the publication and success of such works as Mrs Crowe's "Night Side of Nature," and Joseph Ennemosier's "History of Magic," and similar productions, suffice to show that an enlightened interest is beginning to be felt in a question too long neglected, and which cannot now for any lengthened period be pooh poohed aside by the grave authority of men, who find it more convenient to disown than explain facts which so unmistakeably stand without the limits of their admitted principles. Ghosts, indeed, if we would be just and fearless in our exposition of the truth as it is in nature, must no longer be denied as subjective experiences of humanity. To what further claims, if any, they may be entitled, additional investigation may perhaps hereafter suffice to shew.

What, then, to adopt our usual categorical arrangement, are ghosts—chemical exhalations. the phantoms of an excited imagination, the creations of a diseased brain, or real visitations from the spirit-sphere? These are questions which, under diversified forms, have in effect been put in almost every age, and perhaps in effect received the same answers. For men have from of old been divided on these subjects into nearly the same gradations of scepticism and belief as at present, the principal difference being that the numerical strength of the various schools has undergone a considerable variation according to the dominant tendency of successive ages, which of necessity carries with it the great mass of simply receptive and inherently dependent minds. The recent discoveries of Baron Von Reichenbach, while they have done much to strip the churchyard of its midnight horrors to the scientific, have nevertheless shown that the school-boy who "whistled aloud to keep his courage up" had more occasion for his terrified solo than some rather self-sufficient *savans* once supposed, the recently interred corpse giving birth to luminous appearances visible enough to the duly susceptible, and which have an existence as real and indubitable as Polar radiations from the most tangible of metallic magnets. While the interesting revelations afforded to us by Nicolai of Berlin some years since may suffice to indicate the pathological source of very many visitations of this order, for the cool and self-observant bookseller found that his ghosts came and went, and were endowed with more or less of seeming reality, according to the state of his health, and the efficiency of the medical treatment to which he was subjected.

The foregoing classes embrace an immense number of very terrible apparition cases; albeit an obstinate residuum still remains, not so to be exhaled and dissipated. Of this remainder, however, a large number may be considered as biological. Let me illustrate my meaning in this by a case and its explanation. In a rather dismal lane near a certain village, the spectre of a headless woman is said to be occasionally seen, flitting to and fro, amidst the gloomy darkness and howling tempests of the wintry nights. Of course, every man, woman, and child in the neighbourhood has heard the description of this horrible phantom's appearance over and over again, with every detail and adjunct requisite for giving definitiveness to the conception. So far for the source of the idea, and now for the impression. Polite readers, dwelling in well-paved, well-lighted, well-watched towns, and seeing therein sundry brigandish and ghostly scenes enacted on a beautifully decorated stage, can form but a very imperfect conception of the confused combination of terrors by which the rustic dwellers in a rude country are beset in their nightly errands across dismal moorlands and through suspicious-looking thickets. To these, especially the junior portion, a thrilling tale of some horrible phantom tracking the footsteps or crossing the path of the lonely benighted wanderer comes home with a fearful reality, a terrible intensity, such as individuals less rudely nurtured would utterly fail to realize. The tale, then, of the haunted lane, the troubled dell, the oak where the suicide hung himself, the desolate common where the farmer was murdered, or the stile where the betrayed maiden used to meet her assassin lover, are severally burnt into the very souls of the young listeners, as they devoutly and shudderingly hear incident after incident narrated and dwelt upon with a minuteness that would be tedious beyond measure to all others, but which is devoured by them with a gusto that laughs to scorn the intellectual voracity of a thorough-paced novel reader, arrived at the all-absorbing denouement of the third volume.

The impression, then, is made; now for the evolution. That awful narrative, heard, perhaps, from the lips of one who had actually undergone such a visitation, whose knees had knocked together, and whose hair had stood on end when seemingly face to face with the dreaded spectre—heard, we say, amidst all the accessories of a flickering fire, casting its weird shadows with every varying blaze around the crumbling walls of the old farm kitchen, listened to between the howlings of the storm; this narrative is stored in the profoundest depths of the mind, a reservoir of the horrible, to be evoked from its quiescent slumber in the subjective sphere, and to be projected into all the apparent reality of the objective, whenever a fitting occasion and appropriate influences shall present the opportunity and the forces required for its effective manifestation. On some equally dreary night, perhaps years afterwards, that boy, thus impressed, finds himself alone in the dreaded locality, has to pass the very scene of those horrors at which, even in narration, he has so often shuddered. Association re-pictures them with all the freshness of a first impression, terror adds to the vivid intensity of the conception, previous anxiety or ill health may have shattered the nervous system; and the consequence of all these preparatory and predisposing causes is the terrible presentment of the traditional fiend, clothed in all its supposed horrors, surrounded by all its well-known adjuncts, and pressing on the track or resisting the advance of the terror-stricken peasant, with such a semblance of reality as leaves on him the indelible impression that he too has seen the ghost, or been pursued by the spirit which has long troubled his simple-minded and truth-speaking neighbours and forefathers. Such is the history of most village ghosts; they are the result of impressions transmitted by oral tradition from generation to generation, and kept in existence not by the reality of their visitations, but by the terrors of the seers, whose senses are thus befooled by the visions of an over-excited imagination.

I need scarcely say, that this traditional transmission of powerful mental impressions also affords an explanation of fairy and other rustic tales of spirit-land, in which, it is asserted by the actual seers, that they have beheld and even had conversational intercourse with the " good people ;" the only difference being, that, in the latter case the visions are supposed to be characterized rather by the beautiful or grotesque,—in the former, by the monstrous and fearful. From the effect of various localities on the visions and other experiences of Frederica Hauffe, the celebrated seeress of Prevorst, and from similar results producible, although in an inferior degree, on other highly susceptible sensitives by the diversely characterized mundane influences of different places, we have reason to believe, that many of these village tales of ghostly, fairy, and other visitants, *originated* with sick sensitives, as Reichenbach would call them. These highly, or shall we say morbidly, susceptible persons being acted on by the odic influence of decomposing bodies, and of subjacent streams, minerals, or peculiarly constituted soils or rocks, would frequently manifest the effect of such action by becoming affected with certain visions when passing over the sites so characterized. These visions would generally assume a form consonant with the popular superstitions of their age and country. These sensitives, then, would constitute the primal seers, who, by the truthfulness and force of their convictions, would suffice to impress the more receptive of their neighbours and friends, who, when so affected, might be termed the secondary or biologised visionaries.

Such is probably the history of many a thrilling tale of horror, of many a traditional ghost, whose terrific visitations have troubled the successive generations of some devoted locality. The especial connection of odic emanations with mineral veins and springs or underground streams of water, may also suffice to show the reason why fairies, pixies, and other genii of rustic lore were often said to nocturnally arise from and return into the ground, to haunt mines and other subterranean localities, and to be sometimes incapable of crossing a water-course. All this is exactly what we should expect on the supposition that popular mythology on this subject is but the idealized embodiment of the real experiences of odic sensitives, cast of course in the mould of prevalent belief. The same explanation will also apply to the presumed habit of certain elfish beings, acting as the time-honoured custodiens of buried treasure, this being also productive of odic emanations, more or less perceptible to highly sensitive natures. Even the supposed dancing of these little creatures in the moonlight is probably based on the now admitted fact of a powerful lunar influence, which, though much greater in the tropics than in our temperate zone, is nevertheless sufficiently potent even here to render the changes of " fair

Cynthia " a source of pleasurable or painful emotion to many susceptible persons, whose tides of thought, or rather fancy, rise and fall with the increase and wane of Diana's golden horns, without their being in consequence always subjected to the rather inconvenient process *de lunatico inquirendo*. Is not this specially characterized odic emanation also the fact of nature, underlying the pleasing fiction of classical antiquity respecting the presiding deities of wood and wild, of springs, streams, and caves, &c., in virtue of which every distinct place had its peculiar *genus loci*, that is, particular kind of imponderable influence? Let it never be forgotten that the superstitions of the vulgar are an invaluable storehouse of knowledge, veiled and obscured, but nevertheless embodying the result of observations on phenomena which modern philosophers have been too proud or too careless to notice. The transmitted faith of many generations has ever a more substantial basis than mere cloud-land could supply,—it ever rests ultimately on the firm foundation of reality, and, with a deeper insight than we have yet obtained into the hitherto occult properties of things, will be found to yield a wondrous verification of discovery in its indefinitely progressive and onward march.

LETTER EIGHTH.

VERIFIED APPARITIONS.

IN the foregoing letters the subject of ghosts and their rather troublesome visitations was treated of under its more superficial and thoroughly popular aspect. We have now to penetrate somewhat more deeply into the arcana of this rather mysterious question, for it has been shrewdly suspected that guests of this kind whom people expect are very apt, however unwelcome, to make their appearance, and their doing so under such circumstances is as we have seen by no means unaccountable, especially where the seers are of an impressionable character; moreover, from all the attendant incidents of such cases, subsequent verification is necessarily very difficult, in many instances, indeed, impossible. All that can be ascertained by the most careful inquiry is that some additional victim has been affected by the popular delusion—has seen the ghost and been terrified by it. But after all the evidence educible under such an investigation, we are still left in utter incertitude as to the essential character of the visitation, as to its being subjective or objective, and consequently the real nature of the supposed ghost remains as much a mystery as before, or rather becomes with every repetition of its dreaded appearance a more and more doubtful affair, and thus indeed eventually, to the great comfort of all the parties concerned, vanishes not once only but for ever, the force derived from its first appearance to a real sensitive being gradually lost and dying out like the sound of an echo, more and more faintly repeated with every reverberation. But as everybody knows who has at all studied the subject, there are much more formidable apparition stories than any which can be arranged under the above category of village ghosts. There are the verified appearances of persons who at the moment of dissolution have seemed to present themselves to a friend living at a distance, who has thus received the first intimation of their decease. It is of course easy to deny the fact; to a shallow philosophy it may prove convenient; but the exclusion of such phenomena from the list of human experiences, and the systematic scepticism with which till recently every narrative of this kind, however well substantiated, was sure to be received, argued little either for the real expansiveness of our science, the liberality of our sentiments, or—shall we say it?—the courage of our savans. Of all people really afraid of a true ghost story, commend me indeed to a model philosopher of the last generation. You might as well expect a thoroughly Catholic doctor of divinity to be reasonable under the arguments of an evangelical Protestant, as a gentleman of this class to hear patiently and weigh justly, all the details of evidence by which the case was to be substantiated. His mind antecedently filled with antagonistic ideas, warped and fashioned into the superficial materialism of his time, was no more capable of receiving the demonstration than was that of the old Ptolemaic professor in reference to the new system of Copernicus. The one would not hear of ghosts, the other would not look at the satellites of Jupiter, lest he should be convinced. The blinded folly of Galileo's contemporaries has been a marvel to many succeeding generations, but it was not, after all, so great a rarity as some people suppose. There have been even in our own day some men of great and towering reputation, who have declared that they would not be present at a case of mesmerism, and, *mirabile dictu!* would not believe it even if they were. Let us, then, fabricate no more jokes at the expense of the old school-men. Their stout conservatism of intellect was certainly a far more respectable and pardonable affair in their day than any thing of the like kind in ours. They might be deemed courageous defenders of the old, but our contemporaries, it is to be feared, will only be considered obstinate opponents of the new. But this is a digression.

In addition, then, to the village or traditional, that is biological ghosts, treated of in the previous letter, we hesitate not to profess our belief in another and still more awful class, which may be strictly called mesmeric—that is, they are apparitions produced not by a previous impression but a present influence, not by an antecedent preparationof the mind, but an existent power acting directly upon it. They are the result not of a transmitted idea, but of a primal action on the seer. Of these rather terrible presentments there are too many narratives, and these also too well authenticated, to permit of our doubting the fact that the *eidolon*, or spirit-form of an individual, either at the hour of dissolution or in a time of great mental agitation, or its opposite of extraordinary mental concentration or abstraction, may appear to another person at a distance. As we do not hesitate to admit the statement, neither are we afraid to grapple with its attempted solution; so without farther delay let us proceed to a case and its exposition.

A sailor is on a foreign voyage, but one night his mother or sister, or perchance a young lady between whom and the bold mariner, there are, if possible, even still finer bonds of sympathy, wakes up, and behold there stands the visible presentment of the seaman by her bedside, pale, cold, and dripping wet. Perhaps in addition he speaks, and in a sepulchral voice informs the terrified and horror-stricken young or old lady, as the case may be, that he has just been drowned, giving at the same time many circumstantial details of the catastrophe. Of course the date of this terrible apparition is duly noted, and, strange to say, in due process of time " a black sealed letter" but too sadly corroborates the truthfulness of the ghost, by affirming that on the night in question the poor sailor was washed overboard in a storm, or was wrecked and drowned in a vain attempt to reach the shore. Drawing-room scepticism will of course laugh at the whole tale as impossible, but he who has never heard of similar circumstances is simply unacquainted by personal observation with the experiences and feelings of that large and interesting class, the fearless daring of whose hardy sons constitutes the pride and glory of our island home.

. Now, admitting the facts, what is the philosophic explanation of this spectral annunciation of an event actually occurring in the sphere of reality? Can science account for a telegraphic despatch so strangely yet truthfully communicated? Is the problem susceptible of a satisfactory solution, *minus* the real and *plus* only an imaginary ghost? Let us see. The sailor and the lady are in sympathy; they are intersphered, and consequently mental action and reaction between them is possible, despite all merely terrene obstacles, and notwithstanding the utmost possible distance attainable between two inhabitants of our common globe. The drowning mariner struggling hopelessly amidst the wilderness of waters, feeling that his momentarily decaying strength is the sole barrier between him and eternity, concentrates whatever of remaining mental force he may possess, upon the objects dearest to him on earth. He thinks intensely of them, and with all the preternatural force of impending death acting on a mind in the full vigour of its powers, expires amidst an all absorbing anxiety for their welfare, and perhaps with a vehement desire to once more see and converse with them. This fixity of attention, this strength of desire, this outpouring of the entire being on an object, is an act of mental mesmerisation, effected in the case under consideration with all the tremendous energy of a last resolve, of " a ruling passion strong in death."

And such fixity of attention on the part of an operator at a distance has in fact often produced the mesmeric sleep in patients antecedently under his influence. It is no wonder, therefore, that in such a case as the one under consideration the drowning sailor should by a similar process of mental concentration convert the ordinary sleep of his subject into the mesmeric. In this condition, as we have already remarked, lucid dreaming would be posssible, but it would be lucidity, not exactly spontaneous, but attained to under the influence of another, and therefore often partaking of the dominant impressions of his mind at the time. There would be in short a transference by sympathy both of his sensations and ideas. Now, it is the tendency of dream-life to embody its impressions, and project them from the really subjective sphere of conception into the apparently objective one of perception; hence the sympathetically communicated knowledge of the sailor's desperate situation would be imaged forth to the mind's eye of the dreamer in a seemingly actual presentment of him personally, with all the specialities of condition and feeling then most powerfully acting on him. Hence he looks wet, cold, and pale. It is moreover frequently observed that mesmeric lucides perceive distant persons in their visions as if close at hand, space being in very truth a mere thought-form to the ecstatic. Hence also the figure of the far-off seaman seems to stand by the bedside of his sleeping subject, who, horrified at the terrible vision, and labouring to cast it off, suffers so much from agitation, and obtains perhaps such an unwonted acceleration of pulse, that nature, unable to provide for the endurance of so much agony with the continuance of sleep, kindly occasions an awakening. But an image so powerfully impressed is not in every case to be instantaneously dismissed from the mind; it mingles, like the remains of a dissolving view, with the picture presented by the actual senses, and thus the dripping and cadaverous image of the dream stands forth in the moment of returning consciousness, amidst the furniture and other accessories of the bed-chamber, a seemingly terrific reality, vouched for by all the attendant circumstances of a known and veritable environment. The gloomy and sepulchral voice, the cold touch or icy grip of the phantom, are all to be accounted for in a similar manner; they are the ruling impressions or desires of the operator brought to bear with resistless force on the mind of a passive and simply recipient subject, and embodied not in the form of internal thoughts but external imagery. Change the supposed circumstances of death, and you modify the allegorical or more strictly speaking representative imagery, by which the ideas of an expiring operator are conveyed to his somnolent mesmerisee. Hence the dying soldier, or murdered traveller, may be seen wounded and bleeding in the dream-vision of an attached relative at the time of the catrastrophe, and this somnolent revelation be in a similar manner transferred momentarily to the waking state.

Such are a great majority of those real ghost stories, whose occasional recurrence and subsequent verification still sustain the popular belief in spiritual visitations. Others doubtless take place in that peculiar condition of the system of the seer, known as night-mare, in which, with many of the attributes of viligance, a remarkable and morbid susceptiblity to vision is often combined, while a still smaller number occur in the waking state and in broad daylight, these two conditions being rather antagonistic to the spontaneous evolution of ecstatic lucidity. Hence day ghosts are much greater rarities than those which are nocturnal, for night and darkness being the negative aspects of nature, conduce to the impression-ability of all persons predisposed to the trance-life, while sun-light and the active duties of the day are both favourable to the development of a positive and resistive condition of the nervous system.

Some rather curious illustrations of the truth of the fore-going expositions have occasionally been afforded by a similar appearance of individuals through their spiritual proxy, where death has not taken place. There are several well-authenticated narratives of this kind, but in almost every case it was found on subsequent investigation that the original or real Simon Pure was at the period of his double presentment in a very peculiar condition of consciousness, either vehemently disturbed by the agonising fear of immediately impending death, or drawn out of himself, absent, as we should say, in a reverie or a dreamy contemplation of the persons or scenes to whom or amidst which, his mysterious second-self has so unaccountably been present. Numerous and interesting, however, as are the known and published narratives which suffice to throw light on this important subject, fresh data are yet comparatively rare and difficult of access, such incidents being in general carefully kept as a secret too terrible to be divulged, except to those in the entire confidence of the families to whom such visitations have occurred. The pretentious philosophy of a wilful scepticism, alike afraid of the facts and incompetent to their explanation, has so far done its work of darkness. It has coerced the witnesses into silence, under fear of its inquisitorial rack of ridicule. It has driven the facts for a time beneath the surface, but only to re-appear with accumulated force under the reaction of a dominant spiritualism. Its dogged ignorance has denied what it ought to have explained; its presumption has sat in judgment on what it could not understand. And behold the consequence in that rampant superstition, whose germs, fostered in the hot-house atmosphere of German mysticism, are now being acclimated in the congenial soil of the States, whence a flood of pseudo spiritualism threatens to overspread all Europe; this, however, rightly viewed, being but the indignant assertion of its rights by outraged humanity, whose psychic experiences have been so long treated with contempt by modern Baconians, whose drivelling senility of thought allies them not to the glorious Francis of Verulam, but to those mediæval Aristotelians, who preferred the authority of a master to the direct tuitions of nature.

LETTER NINTH.

DEATH OMENS.

THERE was a time when augury had all the characteristics of a science, when a reliance on its indications had all the sanctity of a religious belief, and when its interpeters were among the honourable of the earth, and composed a " sacred college," little if at all inferior to that other assemblage of eminences, before the spiritual potency of whose scarlet hats, the golden glory of many temporal crowns has but too often waxed dim. But alas for the grandeur and permanency of all merely human institutions, the venerable does but too often become the contemptible, till the idols of the past sink into the laughing-stock of the present. So it has been with classic omens and the auguries thence derived; all sensible men having long since come to the conclusion that the whole affair was a cunningly contrived trick, on the part of a talented and politic aristocracy, for imposing on an ignorant and turbulent democracy, too fierce for the open display of rude force, but not too wise for the advantageous application of a little sacerdotal chicane. Did the " *Plebs* " rise in commotion to demand some new or enforce their claims to some old right, then what so easy as to stem the tide of popular discontent not by human but divine agency, and show on the authority of the augurs, that this was not an auspicious time for the discussion of matters so grave in import to the future destinies of the republic. And again on the eve of a battle with a far out-numbering enemy, the favourable indication afforded by the sacred chicken when passed with military rapidity and precision along the serried ranks, has been known to give additional steadiness and courage even to Roman legionaries, whose otherwise dauntless valour, has occasionally suffered a shade of diminution, when oppressed with the unfavourable intimations of heaven. Omens and their interpretations were indeed an important part of the state machinery of ancient, just as reliques, miracles, and religious processions are of modern Rome. It was a bridle in the mouth of leviathan, with which those native born-riders, the upper classes, contrived at times to turn him withersoever they would. Perhaps the charm was worked too often; or its subserviency to merely political emergencies became too clearly apparent, so that even the dullest of apprehension could no longer remain altogether blind to its temporary subserviency to the expediencies of statesmanship. Quite certain it is that the influence of the augurs declined, and the validity of their decisions was eventually questioned even by the most devout, so that at last Jove might thunder right or left, and birds might fly by twos or threes, yet to such a degree of scandalous indifference had the once profoundly venerative Roman people arrived, that both state and private business could be transacted as if nothing uncommon had occurred. Augury was dethroned. Having like many other things outlived its time, it gradually sank from a power to a pretence, and instead of that stern reality which the greatest generals and wisest statesmen found it convenient to respect, it became a convicted sham which the weakest dared to despise. Such was its history as a state engine. Like almost all other governmental levers, it was prematurely worn out by unskilful usage, and eventually broke in the hands of those who had so foolishly overloaded it.

But despite this its political extinction so many ages since, it still exists more especially in the rural districts; having survived the decay of ancient and the revival of modern civilization. Thus lingering on despite the destruction of that heathenism of which it constituted so important a department, and the development of that Christianity from whose priesthood it has ever received such systematic and authoritative discouragement. What then is the foundation on which this long-enduring fabric rests, to what nutriment of tact does this hardy plant of superstition owe its extraordinary longevity? For an account of natural omens as to the weather, seasons, crops, success in fishing, &c., I cannot do better than refer the reader to the succinct but lucid explanation given by the late Sir Humphrey Davy, the illustrious chemist, who, on the now ascertained laws of meteorology, has shown that many traditional apophthems on these subjects are true, and must have originated in a correct and attentive observation of natural phenomena and a refined appreciation of their mutual dependencies and sequences. But in addition to these there is another class explicable only on those more recondite principles of a profound susceptibility in the human system, which modern mesmeric researches have re-discovered and applied, and it may be observed, that it is the latter only which have survived in any strength or exert any influence at present over the educated and intelligent, at all commensurate with what omens generally did in other ages. I will here narrate an instance and explain it, as illustrations on such a subject are preferable to definitions.

The son of a respectable family was serving as an officer in the East Indies. His mother and sisters were one day sitting occupied as usual with needlework, reading, &c., when the mamma was observed to leave the room, which she re-entered in a few minutes, pale and agitated. To the anxious inquiries of her daughters, she replied that some misfortune had assuredly befallen their absent brother, for on going up stairs a few minutes before, to which she felt resistlessly impelled for the purpose of looking at his miniature, carefully locked with maternal fondness among her most precious jewels, she had the misfortune to let it fall : it broke, and the shattered fragments were now lying on the floor. The young ladies, despite their own misgivings, vainly endeavoured to console their desponding parent. She asserted that her desire to look at the portrait was no common impulse, it came on her like an inspiration; that its fall was no ordinary accident, for she had no sooner taken it in her hand, than a strange tremor in her whole system accompanied with a fearful but indefinable foreboding of some impending evil had caused its fall. Friends of the family to whom this was related looked grave, and even the most philosophic awaited the arrival of the Indian post with more anxiety than they were willing to confess. In due time confirmation of the old lady's fears arrived: the young officer had expired of a jungle fever, about the time when his mother's inexplicable solicitude had caused her to take out his portrait, and when her agitation had so directly contributed to its fall. Of course the truthfulness of omens became a part of the family belief, in the strong assurance of which, they bid easy defiance to logic, philosophy, and all argument based on the agreeable doctrine of mere coincidence.

Now, what is the explanation of this strange fact? It was a case of mental mesmerism,—an instance of that refined and exalted sympathy, which can only exist between minds united by the bonds, and intersphered by the influences of an affection, indissoluble save by death. The mother loved her son, and he reciprocated her attachment with all that filial regard, which distance and separation were calculated to increase rather than diminish. He found himself dying in that far-off land, surrounded only by strangers. The tropical heat of that southern climate, as it increased the burning fever by which he was consumed, would only help all the more powerfully to intensify the longing of the expiring youth for his northern English home. While the swarthy faces and foreign tongue of his native attendants, would recall, as by a painful contrast, the familiar forms and kindly voices that had encircled him in the hours of his boyhood. And there, in the centre of those lovely affections, now lost for ever in this world, would stand, to his mind's eye, the venerable and matronly figure of his mother. He was very young—one of those early sacrifices, of which Britain offers so many annually, to the Juggernaut of her ambition for oriental empire. No newer association, no more passionate affection had yet weakened, by dividing, his regard for that revered parent. He thought of her—of her motherly councils, her maternal admonitions, and her impending deprivation. She was the focus of affection—strong in death. By mutual attachment she was within his sphere, and subjected to his influence, which, being powerfully radiated from him, and concentrated upon her, she could scarcely fail to feel it, in the stilly quietude and holy retirement of her domestic circle. She became uneasy, anxious, agonized, her thoughts dwelt with a morbid intensity, on her loved and absent son—the hope of the family—the pride of her mother's heart; and to satisfy, if it might be, the unspeakable longings of her soul, she went to gaze on his portrait. The disturbance of her mind produced the nervous agitation of her body, her fingers refused their office, and the valued memento dropped from her weakened and incapable grasp. Its destruction on the floor was a natural consequence of its fall. The true omen was not in the breakage of the likeness, which was a physical accident, but in the extraordinary agitation of the individual who was the unintentional author of the catastrophe. In this consisted the evidence of that mysterious message of death, which only finely attuned spirits can receive through such a medium. It was a communication telegraphed by agencies coeval with the birth of humanity, and in whose existence, therefore, the earliest generations were as justfied in believing as the latest. It was a natural omen, that spoke to a mother's heart without the intervention of learned priest or skilful augur, and that wanted no interpretation, but such as her maternal solicitude and affection could well supply.

From the phenomena evolved under powerful media in the production of sounds even at a distance, and more especially from the manifestations of the Seeress of Prevorst, and some other especially susceptible ecstatics, we have reason to think, that the popular notion respecting the death, illness, danger, or dire misfortunes of near relations or attached friends, being sometimes indicated by noises or movement among the furniture, is not altogether so groundless as was once supposed. Enough has been observed in this way to induce a belief, that, under peculiarly exciting and evocative circumstances, it is possible for some persons to thus affect objects at a great distance. That this rarely occurs we admit,—media of such power are not met with every day ; and out of the vast multitude of deaths and catastrophes continually occurring, there are accordingly but few of which any announcement is thus given.   But that occasionally a loud knock on a table round which the family are assembled, the spontaneous ringing of bells, or the auto-matic movement, and perhaps breakage, of some domestic articles, have been contemporaneous with some important event, more especially affecting an absent member of the household, or some valued friend or near relative, we cannot doubt, that is, if our minds be fairly open without prejudice to the reception of evidence.   The radiation of odic force, under the high stimulation of intense fear, desire, regret, or other form of mental agitation or concentration, for either will do, seems to be the natural explanation of this weird and mysterious phenomenon.   The motive force is derived from the mind of the individual suffering the catastrophe, and the only difference between such cases as the above, and that of the verified apparitions treated of in our former letters, is that, in the one instance, the influence sympathetically affects minds, in the other, it dynamically affects things ; diversified modes of action however, with which, thanks to mesmerism, rappings, and spiritual manifestations, we are gradually be-coming acquainted, and on which, that new department of inquiry, into which Baron Von Reichenbach has so pro-foundly entered, promises ere long to throw a sufficiency of light, for the effectual investigation of these and all allied phenomena.

These, however, are omens to others, but there is another class consisting of omens to the individual himself. And first among these is the presentment of his double, in other words, the appearance to him of a form in every respect re-sembling his own. Again, there is no doubt that this also must be enumerated among the more terrible experiences of our common nature. The superstitious belief in which the fact is embodied, is more or less prevalent over the whole of

Europe, and, we may say, the world, neither is it confined to any especial age. The Germans term these rather inconvenient twin-semblances, dopplegangers, while they are known in various parts of Britain, as wraiths or fetches. They are considered an infallible sign of the approaching death of the individual who is so unfortunate as to thus behold himself reflected in Nature's magic mirror. This, however, is an error, as there are many well-authenticated narratives, of persons who have thus beheld themselves in duplicate, who have nevertheless survived the fearful interview during many years. What is not a little singular, third parties have also been spectators of the phenomenon; servants, for instance, have let in an imaginary master, who has taken his place in the study, and been there beheld by the real proprietor of the apartment on his return home *in propria persona*. This obviously belongs to the class of verified, that is, of mesmeric apparitions. Such a circumstance could scarcely occur to an individual in a state of perfect bodily or mental health—it is a morbid symptom, and, as such, has no doubt often preceded dissolution. This was of course observed; thus its character as a death-omen became established, and the depressing influence of fear, combined with the severe shock which such a strange circumstance could scarcely fail to produce on the already shattered nerves of an invalid, will sufficiently account for the many instances in which it has been in truth the precursor of death.

An explanation of its essentially natural character, if widely diffused, would no doubt do much to prevent the evil effects of that depression of spirits, which now usually follows an occurrence of this kind. The utmost that can yet be attempted in this way, must of course be considered as the purest hypothesis, ever liable to immediate modification, on the discovery of additional facts. With this proviso, then, I would suggest that the phenomenon in question, seems to proceed from a too free liberation of nervovital power. This may result either from a state of physical disease or from the mental condition of too intense reverie or abstraction. In the first place, due retentive force is simply wanting ; in the second, positive radiative energy is too great—the one would probably be accompanied with a feeling of intense langour, the other by absence of thought,—the original being mentally present where his double is seen. In this latter case, the individual may be said to have projected his psychic self (probably by desire) to some locality, such as his home, before his corporeal envelope, encumbered by matter and subjected to the laws of space, could possibly arrive. Where the psychic double has remained sufficiently long for the bodily partner to have an interview, the state of mental abstraction has probably continued uninterrupted to the time of meeting. Air, exercise, cessation from study, and change of place, would certainly be desirable in such a case as the foregoing, but the depressing idea of fatality is groundless. Dopplegangers, despite what our learned German friends may say of them, are simply symptoms of disordered nervous function, as such they may demand the aid of a physician but certainly require no exorcist.

The popular idea that the howling of dogs, and the symptoms of distress occasionally exhibited by other animals, are in some way connected with, and premonitory of the impending demise of their masters or other persons, is not, perhaps, altogether without foundation. Death by disease has its precursors, its preparatory changes in the functional working of the system, often perceptible hours and even days before, to the practised eye of the nurse, or the skilful observation of the physician ; and that these more obvious modifications are accompanied with or preceded by others equally important in the nervovital or odic emanations of the patient, we can scarcely doubt. And if so, it is not to be wondered at, that the dog so especially gifted with a sense of smell, so habituated to track the footsteps and distinguish the tread of every member of the household by a specific odour, often perceptible to his highly sensitive organs, hours after the influence has been left, it is no wonder, we say, that to such a creature the exhalations from a moribund patient, should convey information altogether lost upon us. He scents the approaching footsteps of the destroyer from afar, and snifts the fatal omen upon the breeze, and thus gathers a sufficiency of data in reference to the coming event, for the direct and immediate action of his unerring instinct. He is thus impressed, perhaps almost unconsciously, with a shadow of the advancing calamity, and in his distress seeks relief by that long and melancholy howl, which has doubtless often preceded the advent of mortality's last struggle. That dogs do often

"Bay the moon,"

and most unceremoniously disturb the hardly-earned repose of our rustic population, without any other cause than their own canine fancies, will of course be readily admitted. But the death-howl is said by those learned in such matters, to possess a peculiarity of intonation, and a certain sequence of notes, not readily mistakable by those who have once heard it from the throat of a powerful mastiff or vigourous stag-hound. Perhaps if our great naturalists or other recognised authorities on dog-lore, would only condescend to observe the facts, they might find that in this as in so many other instances, the popular superstition has veiled yet preserved the knowledge of a phenomenon, which, when properly investigated and understood, may perhaps be found to cast some additional light on odic emanations, and their connection with the human organism in various stages of health and disease. The almost universally received opinion among country people, that dogs, horses, &c., can see ghosts as soon, or even sooner than men, is only another phase of the same great truth, that animals are often highly susceptible to odic influences, and consequently, is another indication that a wiser generation than the present, will probably study their habits more profoundly, if only for the purpose of obtaining from these natural odometers, some farther indications as to the laws which regulate the radiation and transmission of imponderable forces, at present almost imperceptible, except through their effects on impressionable organisms.

LETTER TENTH.

RUSTIC SORCERY.

In my previous letter on the prevalent superstitions of our day, I dwelt on one of a rather sombre and serious aspect, but there are others of a lighter and perhaps more amusing, yet equally instructive character. Such are the ceremonies practised by young people at Mid-summer night, All-hallowe'en, New Year's eve, and other seasons, supposed to be more than usually favourable to mystic invocations. These rude attempts at sorcery, are obviously a traditional remnant of that grand system of magic, which once overspread the ancient world; and light and trifling as are the processes now employed, and insignificant as may be the results produced, the ritual and its anticipated effects, are worthy of some attention from the point of view, whence we have hitherto contemplated these surviving fragments of antique lore. I trust that, as far as we have yet proceeded, a growing conviction has been produced on the mind of the reader, that mesmeric processes, however veiled and obscured, were an ever-present and ever-active agent in the sorcery, magic, incantations, and invocations of other ages. That a subtle and misunderstood power of nature, was the motive force by which many of the facts were evolved, on which, as a small, though secure basis, the cloud-capt towers of a lofty and time-honoured superstition, were subsequently reared. Not, however, to detain the reader too long by preliminary remarks, we will at once proceed to the subject-matter of our present letter.

As in the drama, the romance, and the novel, there is one master-passion of humanity ever appealed to, and on which as a central pivot, the entire range of subordinate machinery is made to revolve; this same important turning-point on which so much is supposed to depend, being no other than that very ridiculous, but nevertheless very grave affair, *love*, so in the no less romantic and poetical sphere of popular superstition, more especially among the young, this delightful sentiment, has ever played a very important part. When magic mirrors were in fashion, and divining chrystals were employed (albeit they have not yet gone quite into desuetude,) what were nine-tenths of the requests preferred to the potent possessors of these most desirable instruments, and who were those who mostly came to consult them? It was lonely, deserted, doubtful, or despairing youths and maidens, demanding at any price to have a sight of their future partners, that mostly supported those wierd old necromancers, with their flowing robes and astrological girdles—who now make such a fine subject for the modern artist. From the palace to the cottage, from the princess to the peasant, the passion and its concomitant curiosity are essentially one and the same, and whether in the expensive and complicated incantatious of oriental or mediæval sorcery, or in the simpler processes of our rustic belles, the same proclivity to penetrate by any means, beyond the boundaries of our visible present, into the clouded and mysterious realms of the future, is still discernible under all the protean forms, which wealth or poverty, ignorance or knowledge may impress upon the invocation. Of the more ancient and learned processes I have already spoken in some preceding letters; we must now, therefore, confine our attention to the ruder appliances, which still survive among our rural population in the remoter districts of the country, not yet utterly revolutionized in thought and feeling, by those most terible wonder-workers, known to this Athenian generation as "existing facilities for locomotion." And, which, by the way, if they had been favoured with a Homer to describe, or some fine old eastern hyperbolist to use them, would, I take it, have come down to us with such an amount of poetical association, as would have amply sufficed to redeem them from the present unfounded charge of being prosaic. But we are becoming inveterately digressive, so to the witches,—Lancashire or Lanarkshire, Cornish or Connaught, as the case may be, respecting whose power to cast irresistible spells on all beholders, no locomotive bachelor, I may here observe, could ever seriously doubt!

One of the most common forms of invocation resorted to by these fair daughters of Eve, is, for a party of "bonnie lassies," to shut themselves up in a room at the gloaming or twilight; and, thenceforward, occupy the time till midnight, in the repetition of certain couplets, or prose formularies, and in the institution of certain ceremonies, which differ in detail in various provinces, and according to the faith, Protestant or Catholic, of the celebrant priestess. These rites being duly performed, each member of the company proceeds alone into the yard, garden, field, or orchard, attached to the house, and, there, after the repetition of another invocation, and the hurried performance of another ceremony, expects to see the form of her future husband—and I have no doubt that many have done so!

Let us explain the matter, and its apparent incredibility will vanish. A bevy of rustic maidens, all accustomed to go to bed early, sit up late, thus the nervous system becomes a little strained, and there is either over or under tension, according to the mental or physical constitution of the patient. They are all a little flurried with intense expectancy, amounting in many cases to painful apprehension as to the impending event; here we have another source of nervous disturbance. They are all a little conscience-smitten, feeling that what they are about to do is very wrong, for both priests and ministers preach and exhort against all such "vain, foolish, and even sinful attempts to pry into futurity;" here is another source of morbid action. Their attention has for some hours been forcibly concentrated on one subject,—to such a mental condition they are unaccustomed,—and so it rather fevers, flutters, and agitates the fair thaumaturgists! The minds of most have, doubtless during the intervals from one repetition of the ritual to another, been moderately well occupied in thinking on some one happy and favoured youth, whose image is thus vividly present to their inner consciousness. The vestal circle is now fully prepared for any thing of the visionary order, and each one, alone, always an additional source of nervous impressionability to the sensitive, rushes out of a warm and generally over-heated room, into the chilling night air, and thus physically shocked by the sudden change of temperature, her mind filled with an image and an apprehension, what wonder that her subjective conception should be projected into objectivity, and instead of cherishing a beloved image in the innermost sanctuary of her maidenly heart, that she should seem actually to behold it as a pleasing yet terrible phantom, amidst the realities of the outer world. The dear creatures are in truth biologised, only instead of being impressed by an operator, they are so by a *ceremony*, which, as Spanish courtiers of the good old school well knew, is a matter that only the ignorant and superficial ever think really insignificant. The wonder is not that here and there a venerable country dame may be found, who will solemnly assure you that she did, " in the days of auld lang syne," thus actually see "John Anderson, my joe " before they were united, but that the cases are not more numerous where vision has resulted from the use of such exciting processes. An invocation more energetic, a will more determined, a faith more confiding, or an apprehension more horrifying, in short an impression more profound or a susceptibility more acute, is all that is needed for changing the scene of this ghostly interview from the garden to the room, when the dreaded lover stalks into the chamber of horrors to the unutterable dismay of his expectant fair one! This is simple magic, the phenomena evolved being wholly of a subjective order. Let us now advance to that which is higher, and where there is "action at a distance."

A young lady conceives she has been aggrieved by some gentleman, who, perhaps, with the proverbial fickleness of favoured lovers, has exhibited unmistakable symptoms of transferring his attentions to some other less deserving object. She, after due consultation with her female friends as to the most appropriate procedure in this case of male delinquency, at last determines on " working a charm ;" not apparently in the least conscious that she is herself an ever-present and irresistible talisman, more potent than all the laboured exorcisms that necromancer ever uttered, than all the " elixirs of love " that wizard ever compounded ! But this is beside the matter. So let us proceed with all due gravity in unfolding the Isiac mysteries of maidenly potentiality in the occult arts, or rather gentle reader shall we say *hearts*, vastly the more germane we think to the subject matter of our present most learned dissertation ! She must be alone. Who shall describe the power of solitude over a lonely and deserted heart ! No wonder fairy fancies sometimes take the semblance of realities, by a magic which every age has instinctively developed. She must wish intensely to affect the person who is the object of her thoughts, who, unhappy wight, thus becomes the focal point of an indignation, sufficient to thaw the doubly frozen heart of even a faithless Nova Zemblian or erratic Esquimaux. Her attention is generally concentrated by the use of some object used as the representative of her lover, and which thus becomes the medium of transference, such as a waxen image for his body, a pigeon's, or more correctly, *dove's* heart for that indurated callosity, which passes for such an organ in his unprincipled bosom ! These requisite instrumentalities being duly provided, the indignant damsel forthwith proceeds to melt the waxen image before a fire, or in the case of a heart, to stick it full of pins or needles, and then expose it to an equally incovenient degree of caloric. The analogy of those traditional processes is sufficiently obvious,—the fire is doubtless intended to light up that of love or conscience, or perhaps both at once ; while the pins ! truly the darts of Cupid, were nothing to them. Who would not rather be exposed to a whole quiver full of such amatory missiles, than be the object emblematically represented by that little rotatory offering to Hecate, slowly consuming between a fire of best Walsend on the one hand, and of disappointed hopes on the other ? Our military friends may talk of cross fire, and masked batteries, and so forth, but their experience in such matters must be trifling indeed, if they have never been exposed to such a discharge of disciplined fury as we have been just describing. Now it has been narrated as a well-authenticated fact, of course from that most veracious individual " our own correspondent," that under such a combination of circumstances or rather influences, the repentant beau has suddenly made his appearance " in the midst," sometimes *in propria persona*, and sometimes by his psychic proxy, that double to whom we have already alluded in a previous paper, and again let us repeat our shibboleth, " we believe it " ! Start not in unaffected amazement, Oh ! most philosophic peruser of these recondite revelations of the worship of Eros, we mean not to transcend the limits of nature, in our attempted exposition of such weird phenomenon. The lady and gentleman in this case are intersphered. Mesmeric action and reaction is thus possible between them, despite distance. By concentration of thought, the former acts on the latter, sometimes so powerfully, that if near, he is irresistibly attracted to the once cherished object of his fondest hopes, and so knocks at the door or taps at the window just when he is wanted! and a reconciliation is of course affected ; and the " happy couple " can, if they please, tell the tale to their children's children. But should half a kingdom intervene, even an express train would scarcely suffice for the emergency. What then is to be done. He thinks and thinks, and dreams and regrets, and gradually falls into a reverie, in which he becomes oblivious of his present environment, and vividly conscious of another in which his fair inamorata constitutes the principal figure. With her he is mentally present though *corporeally* absent. He now re-acts on her, and when " the charm " is successful this process of interaction proceeds so far as to produce vision on her side, sometimes also on his, both being essentially subjective in origin, though apparently objective in character. Such a phenomenon as the one we have been describing is of course rare, but that it occasionally occurs as a fact is what only the

untravelled or inexperienced would be prepared to deny. It
implies a concentration of thought on the part of the lady,
and a degree of susceptibility on that of the gentleman by no
means common, together with an amount of interspheration
seldom attained between even "the most finely attuned souls.'
That of such rather peculiar experiences, a vivid and, in some
instances, painful recollection should sometimes remain, is not
to be wondered at; and hence, probably, the popular idea
that a lady who has "worked such a spell," ought to keep
her own counsel, and never inform her goodman of the
processes employed for securing his roving and mutable
affections.

The pulling of straws, dipping the fingers into water, and
other amusements so charmingly described in the "Hallow-
e'en" of the immortal Ayrshire ploughman, belong to the
old class of superstitions connected with the *sortes* or *lots*,
and have nothing to do with that evocation of the faculty of
vision, or that interaction at a distance to which we have
been alluding. But where a voice is supposed to be heard,
or a touch felt, we may always, on a sufficiency of evidence,
be prepared to accredit the narration, as a truthful statement
of subjective experience; but we may also be equally prepared to explain it, without having recourse to the exploded
hypothesis of the supernatural.

To the student of antiquity it may perhaps prove interesting to know, that these mystic ceremonies not only date
from a remote period in our own country, but that they are
also connected with, and are probably a remnant of the worship of that female divinity, who, as Bona Dea, Cybele,
Hecate, Isis, and Devee, has in successive ages received the
homage of Romans, Greeks, Egyptians, and Hindoos. Among
the latter, the festival of "Nuvee Patree," or the nine nights,
is still preserved, in the mystic rites attaching to which,
Waren, or extasy, is sought and generally attained by some
one of the ladies assembled, who thereupon becomes the
oracle of the circle, and is said to vaticinate with considerable correctness in reference to domestic and marital affairs

for the next twelve months. Who, prior to the investigation, would have suspected that a rustic ceremony in Christian Europe was but a faint repetition of rites, with which the most formidable of Heathen deities was, and still is, seriously worshipped.

LETTER ELEVENTH.

MIRACLES OF THE PAPAL CHURCH.

INTRODUCTION.

AMONG manifold forms of belief in the supernatural which
have prevailed at various periods, few have been more productive of important results than that which during so many
ages has flourished in Europe, under the sanction and authority of the Roman Church. The lives of her more eminent
saints are a tissue of miracles, to which their death, so far
from putting a period, has rather lent additional force and
lustre by portents wrought at their tombs, and cures effected
by their reliques. For fully fifteen hundred years this unbroken current of marvels has enriched the coffers and rein-
vigorated the waning influence of an ecclesiastical system,
which to a considerable extent, through such instrumentalities,
has been enabled to survive the wreck of one form of civilization, and the antagonistic development of another. And
whose decadent power, when apparently at its lowest ebb,
has again and again risen to its ancient flood-marks, not
simply by the admirably executed manœuvres of hierarchial
strategy, but also by the overwhelming and fanatical enthusiasm so often generated in the minds of a devout but
ignorant laity, by the exhibition of wonders purporting to be
results of a special and direct intervention on the part of
spiritual agencies, for the express purpose of demonstrating to
an unbelieving world, the doctrinal truth and rightful supremacy of the ancient Church.

The peculiarity of many of these wonders is, that they are
not done in a corner—not executed in packed meetings—but,
on the contrary, are accomplished in the open day—such are
the cures at the tombs of saints; and even where, from the

nature of the achievement, few were of necessity its witnesses, at any one time, it is generally found to be of that recurrent order, that an immense amount of corroborative testimony is eventually accumulated to substantiate the testimony proffered in any one individual or isolated case. Such are the occasional luminosity and lightness of body in living saints, their preternatural fasts, their being effected by the stigmata, their prophetic annunciations subsequently verified; and last, though not least, their occasional appearance after death to the faithful, still warring with the trials and temptations of earth. That these extraordinary manifestations were once universally received as genuine miracles, and that the legends in which the narratives of their occurrence are embodied still claim, and in millions of instances receive, the unhesitating belief of many comparatively enlightened members of the Roman Church, we cannot doubt. These minor marvels of thaumaturgic potency may be true or false, but the still greater marvel, the collective wonder, in which all these mere aids or accessories are focalised, is this now present and substantive fact with which we are contemporary, namely, the professed belief of more than one hundred millions of our fellow-Christians in these same incredibilities. There is the true wonder, that " good men and true," full of that energy and power, both of body and mind, which we so complacently flatter ourselves is peculiar to Europeans and their descendants, do despite all sense, common or uncommon, place veritable and reliant faith in these things. Truly the luminosity of a saint or the winking of a Madonna is of marvellously small account in the great scheme of human affairs, as compared with the awful fact that men have, during forty generations, been found willing, and we may say able, to live and die by such portents.

These supposed miracles are, however, a humanitarian tradition; they have come down to us from the remotest past, and are still in existence, as the chief support of old, and the principal propagandist force of new opinions. We may observe them in the incipient bud of barbarism, or in the seer and yellow leaf of a decadent civilisation, for the Caffre prophet and Turkish dervish are ecclesiastical wonder-workers, too infantile or too effete for the effective display of their thaumaturgic power, on the same gigantic scale as that which once throned the mystic hierophants of Egypt in their templed palaces on the Nile. And at this very day, while the Popish priest refers with triumph to the power of reliques, and recounts to his listening flock the wonders they have performed and the manifold excellences they possess, the Mormon missionary, with equal confidence, and fully proportionate success, loudly trumpets forth the cures achieved by the hands of his living saints, and the visional wonders still daily vouchsafed to the more eminent of his prophets. And the people believe. Aye, there is the turning point of the whole matter. Little need any sensible man care for the monstrous legends which slumber in the dusty tomes of sacred biography, were it not that these spirits come forth from their charmed repositories, and stand and gibber in the light of day, a ghastly spectacle of antiquated superstition exhumed for the occasional exigencies of a failing system, and by its satellites thus impudently thrust in the face of all the literature, philosophy, and " general enlightenment" on which this nineteenth century so pre-eminently prides itself. Verily, those who pull the wires of all this ghostly puppetry, must be vastly amused at our marvellous self-complaisance, ever glorifying itself by haughty comparisons of present intellectual luminosity with the crepusculur condition of former "dark ages." Let us, we say, in all modesty, get rid of bleeding pictures, and stigmatised Adolleratas, before we venture on the amiable task of criticising and despising our far off, but no doubt very sensible and worthy progenitors! With the holy coat of Treves not half a generation behind us, silence on the failings of other times, were assuredly more befitting than that tone of supercilious contempt wherewith the misdirected veneration of mediæval worship is now treated. People did but proceed then on the principles of thought and action which they are fain to adopt now, namely, a supposed reliance on their own senses, and a certain dependence on what was conceived to be the credible testimony of others. What, then, do we mean? Why, simply that the marvellous traditions with which all priestly systems of religion, from the Brahminical to the Roman, abound, are based on facts exaggerated and misapprehended, and that, consequently, beneath all the manifold wrappages and disfigurements of their popular legends, the eye that brings with it the power to see, may even now behold the unadorned and unperverted truth, in short, the fact in nature, comparatively small and insignificant, perhaps, but on which, nevertheless, the tremendous superstructure of tale and legend has been gradually erected by the self-imposed and therefore joyful labour of successive generations. We hold that the traditional lumber of every effete system is a growth which, with all its deformities and encumbrances, is a product as natural as the ivy which encircles the aged tree or the dismantled tower, casting the weird spell of its gloomy beauty around the severe and majestic grandeur of power in decay, and returning as with a grandchild's grasp, the failing support of venerable decrepitude.

This is an important question. Protestants deny, and Romanists assert, the truth of those legendary marvels, on which the latter, to some extent, base the claims of their church to be the living recipient of that divine spirit by which our faith was founded, and the promise of whose continuance is said to be thus fulfilled by the miraculous manifestations yet occasionally vouchsafed to the more eminent believers within her pale. The controversy, indeed, so far as this point is at issue, seems to be maintained on the Protestant side, simply by the strength and repetition of negative assertion; always an unsafe procedure. As a preventitive to Romish conversion by the instrumentality of these asserted or exhibited marvels, indeed, the ruder method of our early reformers, who, without caring to deny or examine, roundly asserted that they were effected by the devil, was by far the more secure and effective process. To deny is always safe, while you can get people to believe your denial; more-

over, it is a short, easy, and very convenient way of getting
rid of all uncomfortable instances, and hence, no doubt, the
general resort to it by unbelievers, at all times and in relation to all faiths. But supposing the marvel be a fact, and
withal a reproducible and marketably exhibitible fact, what
then becomes of your foolish counter assertion; verily, it is
used as the best firewood to keep the furnace of your
opponent boiling, who, upon your own showing of the impossibility, loudly claims for his rare phenomenon all the high
prerogatives and privileges of a true miracle. And thus, if
we mistake not, it has happened to many a pervert from the
Protestant flock, who, bred up in the good old easy system
of unexamining denial (which, sooth to say, is nothing more
than the obverse of the medallion of superstition), is utterly
confounded, either on impartially examining the evidence
respecting Romish miracles, or in perhaps actually witnessing
some rather portentous display of priestly potency in this
respect. Now, if we do not greatly err, the whole argument
in this matter has been made to turn on a wrong fulcrum,
for the real question is not altogether and solely, whether the
Romish and other similar wonders did occur or not, but also,
and in addition to this, whether, granting their occurrence,
they be after all veritable miracles, or only rare and extraordinary phenomena. Supposing the latter proposition to be
proved and generally accepted, we think the young, the
weak, the susceptible, and the uninformed, the impressionable, in short, of every class among Protestant churches,
would be much more safe from the insidious attacks of pro-
selytising agents of the Romish church than at present. As,
in addition to many disparaging comparisons between the
unity of faith within the Catholic communion and the increasing disunion without it, a powerful reference is, as we
have already remarked, at due seasons made to the important
fact, that the one church still evidences her claim to be true,
by the continued and uninterrupted possession of miraculous
power, to which her opponents lay no claim. The comparatively frequent reproduction of portents both in persons and

things—the republication and distribution of the lives of saints and the legendary embodiments of past marvels, together with the unshrinking and open avowal of belief in these things by such men as Father Newman, may suffice to convince us that this is an arm of the church militant, which she finds, by long experience, to be by no means inefficient either for making or retaining converts. A thorough and searching investigation into the character of such a claim, that is, into the nature of the marvels said to be produced and satisfactorily vouched for, cannot therefore prove uninteresting at the present moment, when the long-stilled conflict between the two great divisions of the Church universal seems to be again reviving, and the opposing armies are once more drawing up their forces for a battle, and seriously preparing for the final struggle.

As so much space has been already occupied, although, I trust, not unnecessarily, with these preparatory observations, I must defer treating in detail on the subject till my next letter. Suffice it, then, that a general character of identity is found to pervade the legends of every form of superstitious faith, and that the traditional marvels of nearly every time and people bear so near a resemblance to each other as to indicate that they must have sprung from the same fount. If facts, they must rest on a common basis; if fictions, they must spring from some law of the human mind. They are obviously the manifestation of an all-pervading principle, the effects of ever present forces, and, as such, ought to be as susceptible of solution as any other natural phenomena. If this be so, then being given the conditions of their existence, we should be able to reproduce them, or, if this be not from the nature of things attainable at pleasure, we shall, at least, be enabled to say under what combination of forces or influences such manifestations would become recurrent.

Such an inquiry as the present will, it need scarcely be said, prove interesting, not merely for the passing exigencies of a present controversy, but also as a means by which we may the better understand some of those great motive powers by which the magnificent hierarchial organisations of other ages not only maintained their own existence over wonderfully prolonged periods, but also erected a plastic power over the faith and practice of men, which frequently outlasted the especial form of religion with which these thaumaturgic wonders were connected. Not once only but many times have the sybils of one faith reappeared in the saints of another; not in one solitary instance, but in manifold, have the magical rites of a decadent been translated into the religious ceremonies of a nascent system. Not merely have sacerdotal vestments for the body but also for the mind, been inherited by a living present from a long defunct past. Legends, indeed, are enduring things. They can bear transmigration, and often reappear us if in the bloom and freshness of fadeless youth after the twentieth metempsychosis. It is hard to kill a superstition, we would say, indeed, practically impossible, till whatsoever of truth there may be in it get itself honourably recognised as among the substantive realities of actual existence. Smother up a truth by ever so much of energetic denial, get it as you think most respectably buried, and in some unaccountable vampyre fashion it will arise again from its grave, and if not soon decently clad in the robes of admitted fact, will haunt your homes, and suck the mental blood of your children's children as a debasing and most unworthy credence in the diabolical and infernal. Did Papal Rome deny Pythonic inspiration, then, verily, she shall have it returned upon her in mediæval witchcrafts and diabolic possessions. Does Protestantism deny Roman cures and saintly visions. Then shall she see her flocks ravaged by Mormon emissaries, and thinned by transatlantic rappists. Be assured the truth will get itself acknowledged; has in the end resistless power for self-proclamation; becomes by blind resistance fearfully accumulative; is not to be silenced by any human authority, even though it were the unanimous voice of a whole generation, or many such. Of all earthquakes, there is none like that effected by a long imprisoned truth in its process of liberation; of all trumpet blasts, none are so tremendous as the voice of a newly risen verity on its resurrection morn.

We will then, in our next, proceed to a consideration in detail of some of the more prominent wonders, to which the authorised traditions of the Church of Rome refer, when, perhaps, on an unprejudiced examination, it will be found there was less of intentional deception, and more of pardonable mistake, in the authors and witnesses of these strange narratives, than we in the fulness of our Protestant zeal are accustomed to suppose. And it will assuredly be quite enough for the satisfaction of the most rampant partisanship, if we can succeed in showing that professed infallibility has accepted a rare, but perfectly natural fact, for a miraculous interposition on the part of spiritual potencies.

LETTER TWELFTH.

MIRACLES OF THE PAPAL CHURCH.

SAINTLY CURES.

HAVING in a previous letter prepared my readers for the manner in which I propose to treat the subject under consideration, I will now, without farther delay, enter at once on the attempted explanation of saintly wonders, and other *speciosa miracula*, more especially connected with the ancient church. To enter into all the details of a subject so extensive, would, of course, be impossible within the limits necessarily assigned to such a work as the present. A systematic commentary on some authorized edition of the lives of the saints, such as that of Alban Butler, in which mesmeric notes of explanation should accompany the portents narrated in the text, would be the only effectual mode of grappling with this question, under the form of a minute application of mesmerism to the solution of each particular wonder. This, of course, the reader does not need, and I shall therefore confine myself either to general explanations of each distinct class of phenomena, easily applicable to any particular case, or at the utmost give an illustrative instance, with an attempted philosophic exposition of its apparently authenticated facts

Among the most illustrious of Rome's manifold triumphs in the sphere of the miraculous, those perhaps on which she most justly prides herself, as being not merely vain shows of power, but results beneficent as they are real, may be enumerated her cures. These have been effected in various ways, and under very diverse circumstances. Sometimes, as we have said, at the tombs of the dead, and sometimes by the hands of the living. While at others the mere reliques of defunct sanctity, the sprinkling of that holy water, which the church has in so many cases found preternaturally potential, or even the use of that which, having been blessed once and for ever at the fountain head, has thence flowed forth from some holy spring in a ceaseless current of healing virtue, powerful for good, generally of some specific kind, to all succeeding generations of true believers; any one of these diversified vehicles has occasionally sufficed to work a cure, much too decisive for aught but the prejudice of a blind and wilful scepticism to withstand. All this we most readily and cheerfully admit. We do not presume to doubt the concurrent voice of ages in reference to facts. We have vastly too much respect for the common sense and common honesty of mankind, at all periods of time, and in every stage of civilisation, to attempt the Quixotic enterprise of making our individual standard of probability, an admeasurement by which to guage the admissibility of testimony, more or less corroborated by the consistent witnesses of every generation. But while thus yielding the facts, we may legitimately reserve to ourselves the right of interpreting and explaining them by the new light, which a more advanced science may enable us to cast upon them.

And first, as regards those cures effected by the living, these resolve themselves into the effects of mental and physical mesmerism, either separately or in combination. That many of the Catholic saints were good if not great men and women, we cannot doubt. That they practised, according to their light, many virtues, and voluntarily endured many austerities, and were occupied with sublime and elevating thoughts, to the exclusion of most temporary and merely worldly topics, the entire history of their church would clearly indicate. That they were in many instances zealous, enthusiastic, and devoted, our knowledge of human nature would induce us to suppose. Here, then, we have all the elements of mental concentration, frequently combined with high-wrought nervous activity. As a result of this, we find that many of them were extatic, and mesmerists have often noticed that a powerful remedial agency is developed in patients thus exalted.

Thus mentally and physically prepared for the great work of healing, they were, moreover, sustained by the example of their predecessors, and by their belief that such rare gifts were promised of God to His true church. Can we conceive of a more favourable combination of influences, or could we provide an array of circumstances more effectually conducive to the development of sanative energy? No wonder that their prayers alone, or mental mesmerisation, frequently sufficed to produce a beneficial change in the nervous system of those who were more especially the objects of their good wishes; while the laying on of hands, or the manipulatory application of sanative influence, could, with such pure and exalted operators, scarcely fail to prove of extraordinary efficacy. That the holy oil, salt, or water, blessed, that is, mesmerised, by such individuals, should also become the vehicle of a healthy influence, and when applied to the sick should aid in their recovery, is in perfect accordance with the laws of nature and the experience of medical mesmerists.

So much, then, for the saints, who, for the most part, were admirably qualified to become good operators. Now, what class of persons were those on whom they generally acted? First, those labouring under nervous diseases, epilepsy, insanity, chorea, &c., most of whom were classed in the rather vague and extensive category of demoniacs. Now, it is well known that patients of this order are, above all others, morbidly impressionable, and, consequently, in a more than usual degree, susceptible to the various influences which were simultaneously brought to bear upon them. And, let it be recollected, these consisted not merely in the objective force of an admirably qualified operator, working in full faith, but also in the subjective power derived from an entire belief on the part of his patient in the preternatural character of the remedy, and the divine authorisation of the administrant, through whose beneficent instrumentality it was about to be obtained. Here, then, we have the operator's radiative energy sustained and reinforced by the fervour of religious zeal and the high confidence of a reliant faith on a superior power; while the

natural receptivity of the subject is increased by that dependent confidence in the ability of a superior, labouring in the
cause of heaven and the church, which it has been the aim
and purpose of the Roman communion to so especially foster
in their members. The real cause for astonishment is
not that curative wonders became common, but, on the
contrary, that they ever became rare. The decay of faith
and decline of zeal on the part both of priests and people, can
alone account for the gradual cessation of such hygienic results, ever ready, however, to reappear in pristine splendour
of manifestation, whenever the decadent faith and piety of
the church shall again be duly set forth in the life, practice,
and tuition of her more favoured sons. Those who have
heard the tales still prevalent among the Irish peasantry,
respecting the power of some pious priest in reference to the
"falling sickness," (epilepsy,) will be at no loss to understand, how in other and darker ages, when the unshaken
authority of the church covered her clergy like an ægis, the
possessed of devils became calm at the sound of their prayers,
and those seemingly "sick unto death" occasionally felt an
invigorating influence rayed in upon them under the presence
and prayers of the recognised ministers of religion, from
which, as a decided epoch, they could confidently date their
returning health and ultimate recovery.

It should be remembered that the saints of the middle ages
were the great celebrities of their day. The theological idea
then dominated over every other, and the ecclesiastical illustrations had no rivals in the great and commanding reputa-
tions to which literature, art, and science have since given
birth. The austere devotee, with his repeated fasts and
ceaseless vigils, his extatic visions and extraordinary cures,
was then trumpeted forth from every pulpit in the land with
an efficiency that laughs modern advertising to scorn. While
travelling monks and pious pilgrims slowly but sedulously
bore onward the wave of fame, till the piety and power of
the devoted hermit had spread from the narrow limits of his
retired cell or quiet monastery to every court and camp in

Christendom, and was thus a topic of interesting and edifying remark, not only to the simple peasant, but the gallant knight; not only to the village maid, but the titled dame. A faint resemblance to this widely spread oral celebrity may still be seen in the notoriety of some great Hindoo fakeer, or in the extensively diffused sanctity of some Budhist recluse.

Granting, then, the possibility of an actual mesmeric radiation from the living, and admitting the efficiency of this as an instrumentality for the induction of healthy action into the organisation of a patient, how, it may be asked, shall we account for another large class of well authenticated cures, I allude to those which are said to have been effected by reliques, or at the tombs of saints? Living piety, on all the admitted principles of mesmeric pathology, may do much, but how that which is defunct can be rendered competent to the task of healing, is perhaps somewhat more difficult of explanation. Even this seeming wonder, however, will not, perhaps, when duly investigated, be found altogether beyond the sphere of cause and effect. The result here is produced by the strength of the impression to which the patient is subjected. (He believes that the reliques or the tomb are endowed with miraculous power; and, in virtue of this, a change is effected in his system, sufficient, in certain cases, to induce a curative result. The remedial agency is of a biological character; that is, it is self-induced and subjective.) Let us endeavour to render our meaning more clear and definite to the uninitiated reader. Religious fervour and undoubting faith tend both to exalt the action and concentrate the attention of the mind, upon whatever is the subject-matter of belief. Now, in the case under consideration, this is a curative result, to be effected in reference to some ailment. Now, with what is exalted mental action and increased attention accompanied? Why, necessarily with exalted and increased cerebral action, and consequently with an increased development and radiation of nervous energy, which by attention, is especially directed to some one part of the system more than to any other. The range of such a power, its

capabilities and limitations, are as yet but imperfectly understood, for the science of impressions is still in its infancy with
us. In the old adage respecting "fancy," and its power to
kill or cure, we have the popular version of the matter. This
is that power which medical men, with characteristic vagueness of metaphysical apprehension, generally term imagination,
and with the effects of which they are to some extent practically acquainted. It is the " faith " of that devout antiquity,
to whose more earnest sons it was supposed to make all things
possible. The cures at Loretto, the tomb of the Abbe Paris, or
even by the holy coat of Treves, are easily explicable on this
principle, and the most zealous Protestants may safely admit,
and smile at them. When genuine and successful, they are
effected not by the supposed sanctity of the place, or the
reliques, but by the intensity and fervour of the devotion with
which these interesting objects are contemplated. (The devout
sufferer works the miracle upon himself, and reaps the reward, not of another's self-sacrificing labours, but of his own
enthusiastic and undoubting belief.)

The virtues attributed to the waters of certain sacred wells,
are no doubt in part due to the force of the impressions under
which devotees usually resort to them. This is, perhaps, in
some instances complicated with certain hydropathic effects,
attributable to the frequent application of water to the diseased
part. In addition to this, long pilgrimages, with the exercise,
change of air, diet, and general mode of life which they involve,
must, in many diseases, more especially of the nervous order,
prove eminently conducive to the restoration of health. Our
medical friends know the full advantages to be thence derived,
only instead of recommending a pilgrimage to Caldaro, it is
to Cheltenham, where, instead of being sprinkled by the
clergyman, our fashionable invalids proceed to the pump-
room ; and although not ordered to take long walks on un-
breakfasted stomachs by the priest as a penance for the good
of their souls, they are quite willing to undergo similar painful inflictions at the command of the physician, for the benefit
of their bodies.

Protestant Europe may boast itself of having emerged from thraldom to the priests of Rome ; but if we are not very much mistaken, it has been only an exchange of one master for another, and the infliction or deprivation that would have been resisted with indignation, if psychologically commanded by his reverence, in the name and under the authority of the Pontifex Maximus and their eminences the College of Cardinals, is devoutly received and slavishly obeyed when ordered by that justly eminent practitioner, Sir Fulsome Fiddlestick, on the authority of the pharmacopeia, and in the name and experience of the Royal College of Physicians !

" What's in a name ?"

Oh Juliet how blissful was thy ignorance of the ways of men, either in thy century or in this. Alas for " progress," "outgrowing prejudices," "emerging into freedom of thought and action." Have we not seen numberless cases, where not the ignorant so called, but the educated and intelligent, have at last been so " possessed " by the "faculty " that they could neither get up nor go to bed, eat, drink, or walk, except in precise obedience to their medical adviser. How pre-eminently refreshing to hear such people speak of the slavish submission of the Irish peasantry, and the intolerable tyranny of their ghostly fathers ! Reader, we have lived long enough in the world to know that negroes and Catholics are not the only victims who need emancipation. Albeit the most hopeless slaves are not those who would avoid, but those who court the lash, and pay their whippers with a princely hand for its administration !

To those who are intimately acquainted with the details of mesmeric processes, the illuminated manuscripts of the middle ages are eminently interesting and suggestive. There we see holy hermits, and ghostly fathers, represented in the very act of healing the sick, casting out devils, and performing all the other wonders of medical thaumaturgy, for which their reverend confraternity has been so enduringly celebrated. These rather grotesquely designed, but oftentimes exquisitely finished drawings, seem to have furnished the later professional artists in oil, with a traditional outline for the treatment of such subjects in their larger paintings, in which the attitudes, drapery, and general management are such as to indicate the line of descent, and point out the school whence their prevalent ideas were derived. Now, it is perhaps worthy of remark, that in nearly all these representations the relative position of the parties engaged is that of operator and patient, the saint, of course, occupying the former, and his subject the latter. One of these representing St Ewald the fair healing a possessed woman in the presence of Radbrad, Duke of Friesland, after Bernard von Orlay, was engraved and published in the Zoist for October, 1851, with some appropriate remarks by Dr Elliotson. In part 8th of Cassels' " Eminent Masters " there is also an engraving after Peter Subleyras, in which St Benedict is pourtrayed in the act of restoring a dead child to life, in which the mesmeric character of the proceeding is very obvious. Art indeed, whether mediæval or classical, Egyptian or Hindoo, has, both by the pencil and the chisel, preserved many valuable mementos of this kind. While the present practices of the Budhistic Lamas of Tartary, as so amusingly narrated by Messrs Huc and Gabet, together with the processes adopted by the Bucktus and other exorcists and healers of modern India, may suffice to show that the supposed union of sanctity with sanative virtue cannot be a very recent idea. It is, indeed, a part of that mystic legacy from the past, which has proved so rich a bequest to the ancient church, and of which she has not scrupled to avail herself on every occasion, as a rightful inheritance.

It must not be supposed from the foregoing remarks, that we are prepared to admit or substantiate the truth of every narrative of healing which may be found among the Romish legends. In all such cases a small basis of fact will serve as a secure foundation for a most stupendous superstructure of fiction. This fact science is now competent to explain, and even under equally favourable circumstances, reproduce. And it is accordingly willing to recognise it as a verity, whether in the traditions of Rome, or of Las-sa. Here, too, it meets credible testimony and honest but mistaken enthusiasm, not with uninquiring denial and harsh vituperation, but with an acquiescent explanation, which, while it effectually dissolves the spell of the miraculous, and ruthlessly dissipates the enchantment of especial saintship, nevertheless leaves the moral character of the great and good of past ages unassailed. We can now charitably believe them to have been simply mistaken in attributing preternatural virtue to their passes, pointings and other manipulations; and, without presuming intentional deception, can conceive of a zealous friar occasionally boasting of the matchless efficacy of a relique, a shrine, or a spring, in the removal of some subtle form of disease, to which the ordinary medical treatment of his rude age had been found incompetent. It is the shallow and not the profound mind that ever seeks the springs of action in a gross and perverted selfishness, and thinks to discover the motive forces of great mundane and humanitarian movements in the conscious trickery and deceit of grovelling hypocrites. The world's master-spirits are always enthusiasts, not knaves. They may be mistaken, but they are never untruthful. They may be fanatics, but they cannot be impostors. Humanity's higher instincts and proclivities are never wholly at fault, and the virtually canonized of all faiths have generally been deserving of credit for sincerity, though often deficient in enlightenment. We can now afford to be just to the heroes of the Roman calendar. We know the genus of which they were so distinguished a species, and despite the distinctive peculiarities of their creed, can recognise the fundamental identity of a Simon Stylites with a Hindoo fakeer. And without impugning the veracity of a Shrewsbury, can perceive in his Extatica and Adollerata, the germ of those older mysteries, the Sybils and Pythia of a classical antiquity.

LETTER THIRTEENTH.

MIRACLES OF THE PAPAL CHURCH.

FASTING AND VISION.

AMONG the austerities prescribed by the Roman Church fasting occupies a place much too important to be overlooked. Practised at stated intervals by the laity and secular clergy, it constitutes an element of no mean magnitude in the sterner severities voluntarily endured by some of the regulars; while the narratives of saintly abstinence, which abound in the Papal legends, afford ample evidence both of the popular and authorised estimation in which this peculiar virtue has been long held. The extent to which this especial feature of their faith influences the thoughts and habits even of the careless, and more particularly of the devout in the Roman communion, is indeed but imperfectly estimated by the majority of Protestants. Self-denial has in all ages, and under all creeds, been considered a cardinal virtue, and although the forms which it has assumed may have changed with the varying circumstances of professing religionists, the principle has ever been admitted. The philosophic moralist becomes eloquent on the subject of self-command, and the preacher never fails to rise to a higher tone of thought, as he approaches the exalting topic of self-sacrifice for the sake of duty. From the most savage to the most civilised, the man who can forego ease, luxury, and personal indulgence of any kind, under the influence of some nobler motive, is esteemed as more or less heroic, and is held to have thereby demonstrated his claims to our respect, by this proof of his possessing a nature superior to the grosser propensities and lower proclivities of our animal being. In primitive ages, and in older religions, this idea of the necessity of occasionally and even habitually exercising self-restraint seems to have manifested itself more especially under the form of fasting. From the Hindoo devotee, whose rules of life are deduced from the Vedas, up to the latest exemplar of pious monkery, either in the Papal or Puseyite churches, abstinence from meats and drinks is still believed to be a most appropriate and orthodox mode of effecting that " mortification of the body for the good of the soul," in which faiths of form and ceremony, whose action is rather through the outward rite than the inward spirit, have always delighted. On the intrinsic value of taking tea on Friday without milk, or of the real importance which should attach to a dinner of fish in place of flesh, we, however, do not hear mean to dilate, charitably hoping, nevertheless, that even where such things are practised in a devout and humble spirit, the subject of such misconceptions will not go without his reward.

Ordinary fasts, with their effects, either on the body or mind, we may safely leave to be discussed by medical physiologists on the one hand, and formal pietists on the other. What we here propose is to treat more especially of those extraordinary feats of abstinence, that seem at first so incredible, yet are, withal, so well authenticated, that the most as soon as they receive them for facts, are ready also to admit them as miracles. Such are some of those cases in which the entire disuse of food seems to have extended not only over many days, but even weeks, or where, during the major part of a long life, the supply of nutriment was obviously insufficient, according to the received laws of health, to have sustained vitality over so prolonged a period. And here we may remark at the commencement, that such instances of almost preternatural endurance are not confined to the Roman church, or to communions professing the Christian faith, but abound also in the annals of asceticism, attaching to all the sterner creeds which have ever flourished, from that of the North American Indians up to that once prevalent among the Jewish Essenes. A phenomenon so recurrent then, must, assuredly, be dependent for its existence upon a law, and one, too, which an enlightened philosophy should be willing to investigate and an enlarged science to receive. Now, what are the real facts involved in any case of the kind under consideration? Simply these—intense activity of the brain, from whatever cause produced, has sufficed to greatly diminish, and in some instances altogether suspend, the normal functions of the stomach. The vital forces, concentrated for a time on the nervous portion of the system, have forsaken the alimentary, and hence the usual secretion of gastric juice has partially or wholly ceased, the liver has failed to furnish bile, the peristaltic movement of the intestines has become nearly imperceptible, and the function of nutrition has, consequently, been all but suspended. The extent to which this abnormal condition of the system may proceed, without materially interfering with thought, language, respiration, circulation, or even with locomotion, is experimentally quite unknown to ordinary medical men, who, in the occasional cases of whole or partial trance, that sometimes occur spontaneously in this country, or in the instances of artificially induced ecstacy in India, come and gape and wonder, and utter wise saws like the perfectly uninitiated vulgar, and altogether fail to hide their very apparent ignorance of the whole affair, under the specious verbiage of physiological lore, or the pompous pretence of meaningless platitudes about the laws of nature. In all such cases the healthy balance of power has been disturbed, and the overaction of one portion of the system has been such as to interfere with and all but suspend that of some other. The human or any other organism being only capable of evolving a certain amount of power—if this be almost wholly used up by one function arriving at the maximum, some other has to compensate for this, by being reduced to its minimum. The wonderful narrations of saintly abstinence afford us instructive examples of the completion of this process of substitution, but in the dyspeptic symptoms of the hardly worked student, and the over anxious man of business, we have the beginning of which this other is but the end. For a being whose mind has been for years o'erwrought by the intense excitement of daily and hourly devotion, and who, as a process of discipline, has compelled himself to observe painfully prolonged fasts and vigils, I say for such a being to eventually arrive at a condition of disease, in which nervous irritation is exhibited in suspended nutrition, is not only no miracle, but is simply a fulfilment of natural laws, with which every physiologist is or ought to be acquainted. It is plainly the final result of proclivities, earnestly and perseveringly developed, by encouraging conditions of mind and enforcing conditions of body, under which health has finally disappeared, and chronic disease has been induced, whose form is recurrent or permanent paralysis of nutritive power, and whose result, in the great majority of instances, must have been death. The fasting saint of the Catholic Church, like the Indian Saniyasi, is one of a thousand, the one who did not die in the training under which his less fortunate brethren must have sunk by hundreds into a premature grave.

To do the Church of Rome justice, we must observe, that although many of her celebrated saints were most notable fasters, yet did she never consider fasting alone as miraculous, or the power to endure it for any period as sufficient evidence of the patient being worthy of canonization. In addition to the fact of apparently preternatural abstinence being established, it was necessary also to show the absence of any known form of disease, and the presence of such good works as a saint might be legitimately supposed to delight in effecting. Thus Nicolaus von der Flue, a celebrated Swiss recluse of the fifteenth century, is said to have abstained from every species of nourishment during twenty years, but as his wonderful fast was involuntary, and consequently not a meritorious act, it did not procure his admission into the calendar. Nevertheless, brother Nicolaus was a wonderful man, being, despite the aerial tenuity of his sustenance during so long a period, healthy and capable of going out daily to visit persons living at some distance from his retreat. According to Johannes von Muller, the historian of the Helvetic League, "he was a man of uncommon height of stature, well formed, not broken by age; but his chestnut-brown skin covered only a skeleton." It is said that among his other gifts, he could divine secret things, and see into futurity; sufficient evidence this, to the student of ecstacy, as to his real character. He was a spontaneous clairvoyant or seer, and his fasting was an accompaniment of that abnormal condition of the corporeal functions, which permitted of such a display of exalted nervous action. Peter of Alcantara was also a marvellous abstainer from those ordinary "creature comforts" which inferior mortals find so necessary to their existence. In his case this was presumed to be voluntary, and being also accompanied with lightness and luminosity of body, was invested with a religious character, not accorded, it should seem, to the involuntary self-denial of the good Swiss. As to the relative merits and proportionate sanctity of these two men, we certainly cannot profess to discover the justice of that diversity of estimation in which they were held by their co-religionists. To us they seem to belong to the same category of preternaturally, or rather, shall we say, morbidly exalted ecstatics.

In addition, however, to this physical phenomenon of fasting, the saintly and devout of all creeds not uncommonly manifest another of a mental character, namely, that of vision. Not only did the good St Dunstan daringly seize Sathanas by the nose, when the arch-enemy rudely intruded that very prominent organ into the Saint's smithy at Glastonbury; but even the orthodox Martin Luther also found occasion to hurl his inkstand at the same uncourtly visitor, on an occasion by many centuries more recent. And if St Ignatius Loyola felt himself commissioned to found the goodly order of Jesus, in virtue of a vision, was not also our own Colonel Gardiner called to amend his life in a similar manner. If quantity and quality of ecstatic illumination be the test of sanctity or beatification, Behmen or Swedenborg would probably surpass a large portion of the regularly canonized heroes of Rome, and leave not a few Brahminical and Budhistic devotees far in the rear. Given a certain kind and quantity of excitement, and with some minds vision is an unavoidable result. Long-continued solitude and intense thought, are eminently favourable to the development of this peculiar phase of ecstacy. Profound meditation on a few grand and sublime ideas, and the cousequent abstraction of the mind from light and trifling topics, has been ever found powerfully conducive to the evolution of this form of interior life. Those who have the *Times* on their breakfast table, and who enjoy their daily gossip at the " club," whose discursive studies embrace not only all the " latest publications," but who seize, with aquiline velocity—and we had almost said lupine avidity—on every " dashing article" in the monthlies and quarterlies, the moment they appear; such persons, although no doubt eminently qualified, from their intellectual attainments, to pass a sound judgment on most subjects, would, we fear, prove anything but competent on this. They live mentally in the outward, while visionaries ever dwell in the inward. Your Mahomets and Schamyls indeed prove, not uncommonly, very ignorant fellows, when tested by a thoroughly-trained dilettante. Their small modicum of well-digested ideas may, perchance, serve for that clearness of thought which is so requisite for decisive action, but to conceive of the unutterable absurdity of such men inditing or dictating books ! Alas for the reputation of all respectable and well directed literary criticism ; it is precisely the books of such that do last—when they can be induced to write them. The focalized rays of one devout, earnest, enthusiastic, and original mind, burning deeper into the souls of men than the reflected 'light of all the highly-polished classical lanterns which the collected erudition of the ages can supply. Most mortifying, no doubt, that one sun should so far outshine, and what is more, outlast so many glowworms ; but so it is, and as we cannot alter the laws of human nature, our only remedy is to submit.

A worthy scion of the house of Israel, one Benjamin (though not of Tudela) by name, has, in a most apocryphal work, termed " Tancred," made sundry observations to the great disparagement of Europeans, and, among others, ventured on the bold assertion that the Arabian race has alone proved productive of prophets. To the which, we, in virtue of our undoubtedly Saxon origin, venture to give a flat denial, considering the same, indeed, as little other than an impertinent Judaism. The seer is of no country, race, or age. No creed was ever founded, without, at least, one such God sent. Living words have, beyond doubt, been spoken both in Palestine and the Hadjes, for do we not see their fruits, and still live on their very echoes. But were the voices, on whose far off reverberations the sons of Brahma, and Budha, and Odin are or were content to live and die, altogether mouthless? Whose heroic deeds, and whose sublime and inspired thoughts built up the mighty hierarchies of old, venerable for their antiquity, when the founder of a new system lay a puling infant amidst the rushes of the Nile? Verily, Benjamin, we respect thy excessive nationality, but we cannot subscribe to it. God has never been without witnesses. " The vision and the faculty divine," not merely of the bard, but the prophet, is ever present in every generation, latent, we grant, for the most part. " The piled thunder" waiting for a mission. The spirit ever ready for manifestation, on a due invocation. Did not Joan of Arc foretell to the King of France his coronation at Rheims, and was not her prediction fulfilled to the letter? And in what did she differ from the St Agathas and St Theresas, but in this, that she was evoked into action, while they were repressed into quiescence. Alas, say we, for the man who does not believe that the Sybils and Pythia of other days were something more than self-conscious impostors.

The Roman, then, like all other zealous communions, whether of ancient or modern times, has had its illuminati, whose visions, however, assumed their especial form from the traditional peculiarities of its popular mythology. Where Hellenic maidens, in their rapt hour, would have beheld the glorious and beautiful Apollo descending in the radiant effulgence of divine and immortal youth, the incarnated idea of perfect manhood, the devout nuns of later times saw the beatific vision, and were favoured with a visit from St Michael, clothed in that glory which befitted the archangelic chieftain of the heavenly hosts. And where some idealistic youth, whose Grecian soul had been suffused with the poetic imagery of Olympus, would have contemplated the faultless form of the Cyprian goddess, " star of the sea," rising in nascent freshness from the Levantine wave, his successor, the pious monk of some Latin convent, was overwhelmed with a revelation of the Virgin, robed in the spotless innocence of her immaculate life, as the mother of God. And where the Ixions of classic times mistook the cloud forms of a distempered fancy for the majestic grandeur of the wife of Jove, the purer devotees of later ages were blessed with a beneficent smile from the papal Queen of Heaven. Let us not be too severe on the old churches, either of the east or west. They found ecstatic vision in existence. It was an important part of the moral machinery of Pagan antiquity, to which, as a mighty heirloom of mingled good and evil, they had succeeded. The spring yielded a plentiful supply, but its waters were bitter. They purified them, and in place of the morally objectionable pantheon of the classical poets, they filled the imagination of their votaries with the purer conceptions of the Shemitic races. Art may lament this change, but the paganism of Greece and Rome was effete. It was an Augean stable, and Christianity was the Hercules for its purification. The error of the infallibles, consists here, as in other instances, in the assumption of the miraculous, where as an hypothesis, the natural would have sufficed. We do not for a moment deny, that their devout monks and nuns had such experiences as are narrated in their legends, but we deny that such phenomena were aught other than the results of that exaltation of nervous function which science can produce and excitement can evolve without any recourse to the superhuman. What we say is, that had Socrates been a monk of Mount Athos instead of an Athenian philosopher, his Daimon would have assumed the form of his good angel or tutelary

saint; and had Numa been a Papal in place of a heathen
lawgiver of Rome he would have been directed by the
" Blessed Mary" in place of Egeria. In short, we are prepared to admit that St Anthony, St Francis, St Macarius, St
Bernard, St Catherine, St Brigitta, and others whom we
have already named, were not only honest and truthful, but
pre-eminently good and devout persons, who had all the
visions which they have left on record, and uttered all the
predictions, which it is said were afterwards fulfilled. But
we cannot accord to them any speciality of gift from which
the good and true of other faiths must of necessity be excluded.
We also believe that Pythagoras and Apollonius, Gautama
and Heri, had their visions and previsions, and were perfectly truthful to their own convictions in narrating them.

The real visionary is the last man to play the hypocrite.
He is always an enthusiast, and may sometimes be a maniac,
though he is not unfrequently a genius, and this, too, sometimes of the highest—that is, the creative and commanding
order; but whether powerful or imbecile, he is ever sincere.
In frivolous ages such beings disappear from the surface of
society. They are not wanted, and destiny, or shall we
rather say Providence, is ever sparing of its forces. But in
stirring times, when great events are impending, and mighty
revolutions in thought and action are being effected, they
re-appear, and not unfrequently as the master-spirits of the
storm. At the bidding of one such, the barbarous Bedouins
emerged from the obscurity of the desert into the power and
splendour of the Saracenic empire; and under the leadership
of another, the rude tribes of the Caucasus have, in our own
day, successfully bid defiance to the countless legions of
Russia. The visionary, in short, is not an accident. He is
the legitimate effect of causes whose results have been in
process of manifestation from the earliest periods of tradition
to the present day. His influence on creeds and codes, those
resistless moulds of character, it is impossible to calculate.
He has founded empires, and fashioned philosophies, and
given an impulse to action and a direction to thought, with-

out which the elements of civilisation would apparently have remained latent, and the germs of progress been still dormant.   Visionary and mystic are indeed but terms of reproach for him, whom in the place of honour, we term seer and prophet.   *Your* visionary and *our* prophet.   Let us not, then, be too hard upon Rome, or treat the memory of her o'er-earnest sons and daughters with the mockery and insult due only to convicted shams.   They are a great mistake, fatal to the pretensions of an infallible church, but nothing more.   As such, let us use them to her confusion, but not abuse them for vices of which they were never guilty.

LETTER FOURTEENTH.

MIRACLES OF THE PAPAL CHURCH.

STIGMATA AND CROWN OF GLORY.

IN addition to the wonders, curative and visional, mentioned in the foregoing letters, as attaching to the legendary lore of nearly all ancient faiths, and as having, amidst much exaggeration, a basis of truth—that basis being the facts producible either by the excitement of enthusiasm on the one hand, or the application of scientific knowledge through mesmerism, on the other; in addition to these varied phenomena, then, we have some other thaumaturgic results well worthy of attention, both from their intrinsically extraordinary character, and also from the potent influence exercised through their means over the creed and conscience of millions of men, during many successive generations. First among these may be enumerated the physical changes which take place in the bodies of ardent believers. Such are the stigmata, or marks of Christ's crucifixion, which, it is narrated on credible au·thority, have at various periods appeared on the persons of sundry devout members of the true church. And heie, again, we are met by the indubitable and rather startling circumstance, that whether true or false, such mirabilia are, at least, received as authentic by our contemporaries, not simply as favours vouchsafed to long departed generations, but also as effects still recurrent, and as such to be seen and testified to by eye-witnesses neither ignorant nor vulgar, but, on the contrary, holding such a position, socially and intellectually, as to utterly forbid the supposition of wilful deception on their part, or even of easy imposition upon them on that of others. Such are the narratives published by the late Earl of Shrews-bury respecting the extatica and adollerata of the Tyrol. And such, doubtless, were also the accounts of similar marvels in other ages, which were generally seen and testified to by individuals whose evidence upon any other subject would have been esteemed unexceptionable. Here, again, Protestantism, and we may also add infidelity, come in with their denials, their reasonings, their ridicule, and their imputations of intentional trickery and conscious imposture. One extreme ever tends by reaction to develope another; and thus the over-credulity of devotion has perhaps very naturally evoked the opposite and contrasted excess of a rationalistic scepticism, as unphilosophic in its doubts, as was the unreasoning piety in its receptions. Perhaps the truth may be found in a happy mean between these two antagonistic opinions—science, in short, as a mediator may, perchance, be found capable of resolving the entire difficulty, without casting even the shadow of an imputation on the moral character of either party. Let us, then, first try its capability for solution, in reference to the most celebrated of these holy and preternatural marks, the stigmata.

We have already, in speaking of cures at the tombs of saints, treated, at some length, of the extraordinary effect of deep and lasting impressions. Through the mind an effect is produced on the nervous system—a functional change ensues, and healthy action supersedes that which was morbid, or the reverse. Fits, or other forms of disease, may thus disappear at the tomb, or by the touch of a saint; while they may be induced in one previously healthy, by the supposed visitation of a ghost, or the sudden shock arising from the fear of immediately impending death. Action and reaction are equal; and if you can tell me the exact amount of injury which fright, grief, or any other maleficent impression is capable of producing on the health, then I will tell you the exact amount of benefit which an impression of an opposite character, and rightly directed, is competent to effect in the way of cure. We admit the evil, for too many sad and serious facts are continually forcing it upon our notice; but we ignore, or but vaguely admit, the good, perhaps, for this very sufficient reason, that it is yet rather hypothetical than practical. The doctrine of impressions, indeed, as a remedial or even scientific agency, is yet in its infancy, but judging by its potency under a destructive aspect in accidents, we may at least faintly conceive of its efficiency under that recuperative form, in which future and wiser generations will doubtless wield the vast resources which it places at our command. In the effects of fright we behold an impression potent from intensity. In the results of grief we see it powerful from repetition. In the first case it is sudden in its operation, prostrating the nervous energies as by the blast of a tornado, and rending the fair temple of the mind as by the lightning's flash. In the other it slowly but surely crumbles the lofty towers of intellectual and moral supremacy, by undermining their foundations and consuming their substance. It is the rot and mildew that stealthily saps what with open and sudden force it would have utterly failed to overcome. The wasted form, the sunken eye, the pallid cheek, the fevered lip—alas, who has not seen the successive stages of the fell destroyer, that, as anxiety, disappointment, or bereavement, has thus seized and ruthlessly destroyed his hapless victim. Happy, indeed, are we also if the bright look of intelligence, and the self-possession of rationality, has never in one beloved member of our family circle been, under the direr visitation of fright, exchanged for the vacant stare and grovelling imbecility of an idiot, or the frenzied fury of a maniac. Such are some, among many, of the known effects of impressions, and from these we may estimate the amount of power which can be exerted by the mind as an agent reacting on the body. Let us now, then, apply the data so obtained to an explanation of the stigmata.

These consist, when complete, of punctures round the head, in imitation of the crown of thorns, of sores and occasionally of deep depressions in the hands and feet, to represent the marks of the nails, while some very high-wrought ecstatics have actually presented the mark of a spear in their side. The effect of mechanical or chemical applications—says the sceptic, through whose mind leeches, lancets, caustic, and the entire array of medical appliances for the production of similar effects, seems immediately to revolve, on the first mention of the marks as actually existing facts. Unable to deny the phenomena, he at once proceeds to account for them, on grounds perhaps physically possible, but, it may be, morally untenable. The charge of conscious imposture is one often preferred against religious devotees; but, on an examination of the entire case, its improbability often involves greater difficulties than those which it was intended to remove. Ere imputations of a kind so serious can be received in evidence, you must show that those on whom they are cast are worthy of them. Because convenient to a rancorous opponent, they are not therefore necessarily true; nor, we may add, are facts because inexplicable by a shallow science, therefore necessarily miraculous. They may be true, and they may be genuine, and yet they may not necessarily be preternatural. We believe in the stigmata as appearances which have been often witnessed on the persons of devout Romanists, who nevertheless used no physical means for the production of results so astounding. They were the natural aud necessary effects of a fixed, or shall we say often recurrent idea, acting on an organisation more than ordinarily susceptible to the influence of the nervous system. Now what was this idea? The agonising scene of the crucifixion, impressed in all its horrors, first by a physical presentment of the image, carved, coloured, and set forth with all that efficiency and force of representation for which the Roman Church has long been celebrated in her more imposing ceremonies; next by the fervent and eloquent address of the priest; and lastly, by the frequent and prolonged meditation of the devotee. Let us remember that all this has been frequently repeated, and that a preparation for its ultimate manifestation in full force has been going on during every successive generation, by similar influences being brought to bear ou the parents, more especially the mothers of future devotees, often under circumstances that could scarcely fail to be productive of lasting effect on their offspring. If we have any wonder on the subject, it is not that at rare intervals the stigmata do really become visible on the person of some one of the faithful, but that many such are not presentible in every age and country, during and over which the Papal Church has exercised a dominant sway. As a physiological fact, no law of nature is broken by it, and its reception as such, when due evidence of its actual existence is forthcoming, consequently involves no difficulty, and demands no extraordinary credulity in the believer.

Let us now examine another phenomenon, of which the Church often boasts, as a manifestation of celestial power in the persons of her more favoured saints, we allude to the luminosity by which they have been partially or wholly engirdled or suffused. This mild radiance is said to have been often perceptible, sometimes like a lambent flame, and frequently as an electric or rather odic corruscation, encircling the heads, and more rarely enveloping and even pervading the entire body of eminent and enthusiastic members of the calendar. This fact, although in many instances well attested as a frequently recurrent phenomenon, has been met by denial, based wholly on its supposed improbability. Its explanation, however, is easy. It is simply a manifestation of odic light, in such intensity, as to be perceptible to ordinary as well as to sensitive eyes. To the latter, every living body, even that of a vegetable, appears thus transfigured; in other words, thus transfused with odic force. The higher the life the more intense and brilliant the display. For such a radiation as that which the legends of the church describe, an unusually active condition of the nervous system would be required, such as only high-wrought enthusiasts in a state of intense ecstacy ever attain to. That they have arrived at this degree of exaltation I have no doubt. To project such a halo of glory as would be perceptible by ordinary vision would, however, demand immense energy, and such as the frame could only sustain during a comparatively short period. Hence we read that the illumination was in general only perceptible during the time of rapt devotion, gradually waning with a return of the mind to its ordinary condition. Such is said to have been its character in the case of the fasting Peter of Alcantara alluded to in a former letter. In all probability, the phenomenon was in many instances only perceptible to the partially sensitive—the nuns and monks who, from confinement, frequent fasting, and prolonged concentration of thought, would tend to develope that susceptibility to odic emanations which might render them cognisant of such a phenomenon, when it was wholly invisible to ordinary observers. The halo surrounding the heads of the more illustrious sons and daughters of faith is not altogether a mere figment of art, but is the traditional representation of a fact which, although of rare occurrence, is not quite unprecedented.

Connected with, and to some extent consequent upon, this luminosity of body is also another corporeal phenomenon, namely, its lightness. Who has not heard of some hardly-pressed saint, on some dire emergency, crossing a river or estuary in that rather fragile bark, his outspread cloak? Nay, has not an eminently learned and pious convert to the doctrines of the ancient church publicly avowed and gloried in his ability to believe in the same? So, also, do we; but, perhaps, on somewhat different grounds from those which have procured the assent of Father Newman. We believe, in so far as true, it was natural, while he most devoutly conceives it to have been supernatural. We think it arose from the same force which occasioned the corresponding lightness of the mediæval witches, and by which the archmagicians of various ages have been said to raise themselves in the air, a feat which the Brahmins of the East and the medicine men of the West are reported to still occasionally repeat. That ecstacy under some of its modifications does produce a buoyant tendency is certain; and whether this be sufficient to enable the subject to float in water or in air, seems to depend on the degree of intensity in which the ecstatic exaltation is manifested. A similar phenomenon was observed in connexion with the seeress of Prevorst. It has also been noticed, at various periods, in individuals supposed to be possessed

by evil spirits, but who probably were either epileptic or
insane; and it has been reproduced among the rapping media
in America. It seems to be connected with a powerful radiation of nervous energy, by which the gravitating tendency
is for the time overcome or suspended. It is eminently
interesting as a phase of mesmeric power, to which the magi-
cians of old, and the high-wrought enthusiasts of all ages and
faiths, seem to have attained, but to which the resources of
modern science are yet unequal. I suspect it is a phenomenon more dependent for its manifestation on the internal
condition of the subject than on the external action of an
operator. Hence, like luminosity, it is more likely to be
developed in the excited and enthusiastic devotee than in
the person of one who quiescently and passively submits
to the influence of another. It is a phenomenon rather of
radiation than reception, and must consequently be expected
in the class of self-induced ecstatics, rather than in that of
regularly mesmerised patients.

Throughout the entire range of foregoing wonders, we find
that they are not peculiar to any age, country, or faith. The
supposed miracles of Budhism, Brahminism, Romanism,
witchcraft, and magic, are essentially identical in result,
while the difference in means is rather imaginary than real.
The advocate of each creed, of course, heartily believes that
while the wonders achieved by his saints are celestial, those
of his opponents are diabolical. Thus the Lazarite monks,
Huc and Gabet, to whom we have already alluded in a
former letter, were fully persuaded that the unaccountable
marvels which they witnessed in Tartary were wrought by
the aid of the Devil, but the good fathers would doubtless
have been grievously shocked at a similar scandalous insinuation in reference to the miraculous pretensions of their own
Church. It is the old tale of the cameleon—

"They all are right, they all are wrong."

Nature is the author of the whole. Man holds resources
within the mystic depths of his richly endowed being, whereof
the most extravagant would scarcely dare to dream. And

of all his thaumaturgic powers, the will is the most potent; and this, too, not under the manifestation of conscious effort, but when sustained and led on in its operations by the supporting influence of an expectant faith. Then, in very truth, to will is to do, and effects follow the action of this most potent agency of volition, not by the abrogation of any law of the universe, but by the introduction of forces which, usually latent, are necessarily productive of new and unusual results, when brought out into energetic efficiency. Here at present science is at fault, and must veil her lofty pretensions before the actual achievements of a Tartarian Lama, or a Sheik of Mount Lebanon. Yet we need not despair; magic is but science in the wrappage of superstition. It is the alchymy of the will-power, and when once thoroughly mastered by the men who have evolved the splendid results of modern experimental philosophy, will, doubtless, emerge into a degree of practical efficiency, such as it can never attain to in the hands either of ignorant fanatics or mystical thaumaturgists. The priesthoods of Egypt, India, Chaldea, and Rome, have done much; let us hope that the rising priesthood of intellect, unfettered by forms and untrammelled by traditions, will yet prevail to accomplish vastly more.

LETTER FIFTEENTH.

RITUAL OF THE PAPAL CHURCH.

HOLY WATER. INCENSE. LITANIES.

IN my previous letters on the miracles of the Roman Church I have endeavoured to trace the presence of natural phenomena as veritable realities, hidden beneath the wrappages of popular superstition, and appearing under the deceptive folds of this disguise as preternatural products. To those who have done me the honour to pursue these lucubrations thus far, I hope it has been made obvious that such mirabilia were the result neither of intentional deception nor spiritual intervention; but, on the contrary, were the legitimate effects of physical or psychical forces, operating in strict obedience to the established laws of the universe. As an appropriate conclusion to this department of inquiry, I will now attempt to explain the origin of some rites and ceremonies which the old church has, whether wisely or not, carefully conserved and handed down, from generation to generation, as a priceless heirloom from the remotest past. We use this word remotest advisedly, for it will, we apprehend, become apparent, as we proceed, that the Papal hierarchy is in possession not only of the traditional observances which might be, according to their showing, derived from early Christian and Jewish sources, but also of others, dating from the dawn of religious ideas in the mind of primeval generations. Not, however, to detain the reader, by observations of a merely preliminary character, we will at once commence a survey of some of these venerable rites, with their accessories, when the fact of their mesmeric origin will, we doubt not, be rendered apparent to all whose minds are fairly open to conviction on such a subject.

No one who has ever attended worship at a Catholic chapel can be ignorant of the important position which "holy water" occupies in the estimation, both of the lay and clerical portion of the Roman communion. It stands at the entrance of the temple, and no decently devout member of the church would think of entering within its sacred precincts, without first applying a portion of the mysteriously potent fluid to his person. In all places, and under all circumstances, where an especially sanctifying influence is to be brought into action, the sprinkling of holy water is had recourse to. By holy water devils are cast out, and the young are baptized into the church; by holy oil the dying are sent to heaven, and by holy salt the dead are held to be more assuredly blessed. Whence then comes this idea as to a material agent being made the vehicle of spiritual influence? In the first place, let us remember holy water is by no means peculiar to Christian churches, either Greek or Roman. It was known in the ritual of classical antiquity, and is still preserved in both the Brahminical and Budhistic forms of eastern worship. It is, in fact, the mesmerised water of the medical magnetist, over which passes have been made, and on which the will has been directed. Whether the operator be costumed *a la mode*, or clothed in the flowing robes of an oriental or occidental priest; and whether his manipulations be directed by scientific knowledge, or guided only by a traditional procedure, of which the rationale has been lost in the long descent of almost countless ages of successive inheritance, is of no importance. The thing is the same, though the vesture under which it may be presented seems so widely different. Here, as in many things else, the later faith has inherited the forms, without, perhaps, fully partaking of the potentiality of the primal creed, which, being closer to nature, had perhaps more of its force. Modern science, however, is rapidly effecting the great work of restitution, by stripping the fact, hidden beneath these manifold wrappages, of its gorgeous but cumbrous habiliments, and presenting it anew, to the unperverted conceptions of mankind, in the graceful raiment of a simple verity.

Once within the portal of the sacred edifice, however, the educated Protestant will not be long in detecting other indications of antique life in addition to the lustrations of the font. Should the holy sacrifice of the mass be proceeding, he will, in the rolling clouds of fragrant incense, discover another feature of resemblance to forms of religion either long since defunct, or now existing only under their primeval types in the farther East. The burning of incense has ever constituted an important part of the dignified and imposing ceremonial of public devotion, in all the great sacrificial religions of Asia, that glorious land of aromatic woods and gums, ripened to perfection amidst the shadeless sunshine of its burning plains, and loading, as with a free-will offering of o'er-bounteous nature, the balmy zephyrs of its delicious vales. From thence this graceful and agreeable rite, has been transferred, together with the creeds of whose service it constituted so important a part, to northern and western realms, whose cold and cloudy clime could furnish no fit substitute for the fragrant productions of more genial soils. Commerce, however, has long supplied the necessities of the temple, and the slowly curling volumes of odorous vapour, richly laden with the spicy effluences of Araby and Ind, have still continued to float in their mystic grandeur and emblamatical beauty to the fretted roofs of our Gothic cathedrals. Strange and almost weird combination, this, of the rites of a sunny and almost cloudless land, re-enacted in temples doubly dark, both from the sombre gloom of their wintry skies, and the deeply-shaded light of their richly blazoned windows, where mediæval art so quaintly represented the heroic deeds of ages and races in all respects most widely separated from the celebrants and their congregation. Rome has inherited, and preserved the dramatic power of the past in her public worship. It is a potency of which her priesthood know, and her people feel, the advantage ; and on which Protestantism, after three centuries of sturdy abnegation, is beginning to look with longing and retroverted gaze. But we must not here be tempted into a digression, otherwise the surplices and candles of idealising

Lutherans might, perhaps, furnish us with subject-matter for rather edifying remark in this connexion.

What then, it will, perhaps, be asked, was the primal use, and consequently what the origin of incense, as a part of the ritual of public worship? We answer—the production of morbific effects, or more correctly, the induction of abnormal conditions of the nervous system in highly sensitive subjects, by which they would be all the more readily prepared for experiencing vision, on the application of the requisite stimuli, in the form of moral or physical impressions. Here, as in many other departments, the modern faith has preserved the rite as a symbol, long after having become oblivious of the fact on which it was based. In nearly all the thaumaturgic rites of ancient magic, when either the dead, the absent, the angelic, or the divine, were to be made manifest to the exalted perceptions of the devout, the chamber of mystery was usually provided with a chafing dish, which the hierophant, or his assistant, was careful to keep well supplied with chemical products, whose exhalations were calculated to evoke a susceptibility to visional ecstacy, on the part of the consulting person, who had also generally been prepared for a luminous crisis, by previous fastings and vigils, and in whom expectant attention and a profound reliance on the supernal powers of the magician, also co-operated as moral influences specially conducive to the same result. And it is, perhaps, worthy of remark that it was from the waving folds of the odorous cloud of potential vapour, the desired shape usually fashioned itself at the dread invocation of the mighty enchanter, to the rapt senses of the terrified consulter. The harmless incense which now so gracefully ascends from the waving censer of a modern acolyte was, in such a case, but the vehicle of more potent agencies. The existing rite is indeed but part of the empty and lifeless form of a once powerful mesmeric process, at whose tremendous evocations awful shapes of might and mystery seemed to body themselves forth to the glazed eye of the trembling neophyte. The outer and exoteric ritual, it should be remembered, was ever so arranged as to be emblematical to the initiated of the more secret and sacred rites, through which the most had so painfully acquired their esoteric lore. And it is precisely this simpler ritual for the outer-court worshippers, which is now retained as the very obvious remnant of a pre-existing heathenism, in the older forms of Christian worship, whether of the east or the west.

Holy water and incense, however, are not the only specialities in which the attentive observer, acquainted with mesmerism in all its varied phases, will discover traces of his favourite science amidst the traditional rites of Papal worship. As the service proceeds through the manifold forms required by the diversified occasions of successive seasons, he cannot fail to notice the wearisome length to which the various litanies, with their monotonous repetitions, are often prolonged. Some observations on the origin of this peculiar form of devotion will not, therefore, be here wholly misplaced. As examples of pregnant brevity, combined with perfect lucidity, the sentences in which the founder of Christianity expounded his views have no parallel except in the introductory chapter of Genesis, where the creative fiat, "Let there be light," is issued with such divinely commanding concentration. Whether in his beatitudes to the multitude on the mount, or in his after discourses to more select disciples, meaning is never diffused into platitudes, but focalised into the smallest compass compatible with clearness; while the model prayer, with all its sufficiency, has not one needless accessory. Such was the Master, emphatically of few words, although his message was the thunder-voice of Providence, sitting in judgment on one world, which it was about to supersede, and evoking another, destined to supplant it. "Use not vain repetitions," said he, prophetically warning his followers against that very system of worship which has eventuated in the lifeless liturgies of Christendom. Whence, then, come these observances, it may be asked, so diametrically opposed both to the precepts and practice of the Head of the Church? We answer, somewhat reluctantly, but, we believe, truthfully, from a religion of magic, the oft-repeated spells and incantations of whose mystic ritual are still unmistakeably discernible throughout the whole of this strange perversion of the spirit of prayerful intercession. This, we grant, is a severe sentence; let us, therefore, to the specification. That these " vain repetitions" are not of the Master, is, as we have already said, obvious, he having spoken of them as heathenish; and that they were not originated by His immediate and authorised disciples is equally clear, for their manifold epistles to the Christian churches contain no allusion to any such modes of devotion. They have their prototypes, no doubt, in the later and debased Judaism of the Talmud; but this comes from the same source, it is a part of the corruption introduced into the purer Mosaic system by the heathen element from without. I would say, then, that, immediately, litanies are classical, mediately, they are Budhistic, and, primarily, they are magical, that is, mesmeric in their origin. The derivation is plain, at least to us; let us now, then, attempt its demonstration to others.

In all the ancient rites of invocation, evocation, and other ceremonies intended to produce an effect on the mind of the consulting person, and, through it influence his system, so as to render it susceptible to vision for necromantic, or to initiate a re-cuperative action for medical purposes, the frequent repetition of a given formulary always constituted an important element. Biology is this fact, stripped of its superstitious accessories, and reduced to its simplest form as the science of impressions. The hallowe'en charms of a rustic maid, the muttered spells of a village crone, the more tremendous invocations of a mediæval magician, the oft-repeated orisons of a Hindoo fakeer, and the thousand-fold prayers of a Budhish devotee, told off like those of people nearer home on his rosary of beads, exhibit the successive stages of development in the theory and practice of reiteration as a means for the production of effects by the accumulation of power. Of the efficiency of this moral leverage we do not doubt, of its propriety we shall not here presume to speak; its origin and descent are all with which, from the nature of these remarks, we need here concern ourselves. Originating, then, we would say, in the Magian rites of primeval ages, litanies were, at a period long anterior to authentic tradition, transferred from the sanctum, where, with due accessories, they were really potent, to the popular ritual, where they were simply symbolical. Constituting thus an important part of the public worship of all the older religions of the East, they were, with them, and their derivative forms, transplanted into Europe, where they still survive in a degree of power and respectability, which laughs to scorn all attempts at modification, and threatens to bid defiance to the press and the telegraph for centuries.

In addition to the foregoing, there is another subject to which we would wish to direct the reader's attention, although we approach it with some hesitancy, lest the real spirit and purpose of these letters should thereby become the subject of grave misapprehension. We allude to the rite of confirmation, in which the phrenomesmeric act of placing the hand on the region of the moral principles, and so providing a *quasi* stimulation to veneration, conscientiousness, benevolence, &c., is so beautifully suggestive of exalted manifestations, evoked in accordance with the newest discoveries of science. Tha, this is a traditional process, handed down from the older initiations, we can scarcely doubt; for, although we have reason to believe that phrenology, in its detail, was unknown to the earlier generations, yet from intuition, or perhaps the ecstatic revelation of their seers, they seem to have attained so far to a practical acquaintance with the fact, as to have originated the rite of the confirming hierophant placing his hand on that part of the head, which a modern mesmeric operator excites, when he wishes to evoke a promise from his subject to be afterwards fulfilled unconsciously in the waking state. Now there are some indications that, of old, the highest forms of initiation were seldom attained to but by Neophytes, who had become so far intersphered with their superiors as to be virtually under their mesmeric influence. We may see a remnant of this among the Buchtus of modern India, who take care to be always surrounded by disciples, rendered so susceptible to the trance-state, that they can be at any time thrown into it at the pleasure of their principals. There are those who conceive that Chiron and the Centaurs generally were hierophants of this order, and who fancy they can detect faint traces, or rather indications, of something similar in the Orphic and Pythagorean fragments. Be this, however, as it may, the mystery of mesmeric initiation has certainly prevailed from time immemorial in the east, that primal home of western faith and practice. The reality then, it seems, concealed under this rite, was a solemn promise of secrecy as to the lore communicated, of faithfulness to the order of which he had been admitted a member, and of devotion to the cause with which he was now connected, all exacted from the initiate while under some form of mesmeric influence, whereby his steadiness to the vow might be rendered more probable, under all the varying circumstances of future trial and temptation. Here, then, we may again see the purely inoperative and merely outward and symbolical rite, preserved in the forms of a later creed, while the effective fact of which it was so suggestive to the initiated has been lost in the night of ages.

I might, were it required, go more into details on this subject, and point out the obvious traces of a mesmeric origin in many other ceremonies attaching to the Roman, and directly derivative communions. Some of these mystic rites have passed from the hands of the priesthood, and are now the inheritance of the people. Such are the processes, manipulatory and otherwise, by which a devout Catholic mother blesses her infant before committing it to rest. The manifold touchings, crossings, and other arrangements, for insuring frequent contact between the maternal hand and various parts of the body of the child amount, in fact, to a system of traditional mesmerism for nursery purposes; and after witnessing it, I was quite prepared to hear that the little responsibilities slept all the better for its application. I could wish indeed that more enlightened (?) Protestant mammas would resort to a similar instrumentality, in place of those narcotics, which are, in reality, more noxious than all the saints in all the calendars, "from Britain to Japan!" But we have been, perhaps, already sufficiently diffuse on a subject with the minute facts of which Protestant readers must of necessity be but imperfectly acquainted, and so will hasten to conclude this rather prolonged series of letters with a few words in the way both of explanation and exculpation.

I trust that the spirit which has dictated these communications will not be mistaken. In my remarks on Papal portents, my purpose has been to demonstrate the presence of a natural fact where the Romanist has presumed the existence of a miracle, and the Protestant has suspected an imposition. Conceiving both parties to be mistaken, and believing that truth, however unpleasant, is always preferable to misconception, I have endeavoured, while substantiating the reality, to strip it of its disguises. Should the views herein advocated be correct, Rome, while losing her claims to preternatural power, will still retain a character for intentional veracity. Her legends, while demonstrating fallibility in the reception of natural phenomena for spiritual marvels, will yet leave her untouched by the accusation of wilful deception. We may pity her weakness, but shall not need to detest her untruthfulness. We may smile at her mistakes, but need not become indignant at her impositions. If this be so, the zealous Protestant now knows his true weapon, not denial, but explanation. Fanaticism may lament, but charity will rejoice at this solution; for it liberates a venerable communion and their numerous clergy, from a slander of which we cannot but rejoice to relieve the partakers of our common faith. As to the mesmeric origin of a ritual now applied to other purposes I am not aware that this would constitute any valid ground of objection to its continued use, provided this were considered in other respects desirable. The controversy on this subject must, therefore, still proceed on its former data. The more enlightened Romanists are, I believe, already prepared to receive a rational solution of marvels, which they have long considered rather an onus than an honour to their church, and while surrendering her infallibility on this point, will still defend it in reference to doctrine, to which alone the more logical conceive this great prerogative to apply. In fine, I wish it to be clearly understood, that these letters are simply attempted expositions of scientific truth, and, as such, at the farthest possible remove from the sphere of religious controversy, and that *odium theologicum* to which it seldom fails to give birth. I know from personal experience too much of the virtues happily still to be found in every branch of the Christian Church, to treat the tenets, rites, or individual members of any sect with intentional disrespect. In the pursuit of truth, the conclusions maintained in the present and preceding letters have forced themselves on my mind. If, in stating them, I should have wounded the feelings of any members of so large a body of our co-believers, as those attached to the Church of Rome, I am sorry; but I can assure them it is from no want of power to appreciate those manifold excellencies of character, which, in a lengthened residence among them, I have found to be as richly developed under their peculiar tuition, as under that of any other Christian body with whose communicants I have had the honour to be acquainted.

THE END.